Contents

The long familiar names have been used here although reclassification now places mollies and guppies in the genus *Poecilia*.

Introduction

The Poeciliidae, or viviparous tooth carps, are fishes which bear living young. They are very well known to aquarists and are represented by the platy or moon fish *(Xiphophorus maculatus)*, the swordtail, *(Xiphophorus helleri)*, the mollie *(Mollienesia* species), and, of course, by the guppy, *Lebistes reticulatus.* There are, in addition, many other live-bearing fishes of importance to aquarists.

This family is found only in the Americas and is remarkable in a number of ways. Many species, including the guppy and mollie, readily acclimatize to brackish or even completely marine water and can thus readily populate new areas via the coastline. It is interesting, however, that they have not succeeded in migrating from the American continent except to nearby islands. Thus, they are found in the West Indies, and the guppy comes from Trinidad. These fishes have been domesticated for a long time, with the result that they are now available to fanciers in considerable variety. Platys and swordtails come in a great variety of colors and during recent years, many new finnage types have been evolved. Although these fishes are characteristically deeply colored all over the body, it has only been with great difficulty that breeders have been able to produce strains of guppies of a similar color texture. The original guppy used to be known as the millions fish because not only did it exist in nature in very large numbers, but also because no two fishes looked alike.

The guppy is characteristically a piebald fish with multi-colored body, tail, and fins, and with a very great propensity for variation. It was first introduced into Europe as an aquarium fish in 1908 and is said to have reached the United States in 1912. It has thus a history of more than 50 years as an aquarium fish and if one realizes that several generations of guppies can be raised per year, this may be the equivalent of 100 to 200 generations. As a result, the guppy in domestication has passed the point at which an outburst of a great variety of different mutant types occurs mainly as a result of varying degrees of inbreeding. This is a characteristic of all types of animal under domestication. It is seen in various members of the *Poeciliidae*, but perhaps in greatest profusion in the guppy. This phenomenon is also seen in other domestic animals such as the dog and the budgerigar, both of which have been bred for a considerable period with a view to producing different varieties. As we shall see in a later section, there has been a bigger outburst of new guppy varieties during the past decade than has ever occurred before. This has in its turn been caused not only by an increase in the total number of aquarists who are trying to produce new guppy strains but also because many of them changed their methods of doing it.

The guppy is named after its discoverer, Rev. Lechmere Guppy. More correctly, he would appear to have been the rediscoverer of the guppy; but as far as aquarists are concerned, he was the first to introduce it to them and thus discovered it as an aquarium fish. It rapidly became a laboratory fish kept and studied by geneticists, by embryologists, and by many other students of ichthyology, because the guppy is in many ways a particularly suitable fish for scientific study. Its live-bearing habits needed investigation, and study of the manner of procreation has resulted in some fascinating discoveries, while its genetics were found to be of great importance.

Schmidt and Winge in Denmark were among the first to undertake extensive studies of genetics in the guppy. They were able to establish that sex determination is normally dependent on a single pair of sex chromosomes but that these were not as permanently fixed in their function as are the corresponding sex chromosomes of higher vertebrates. Thus, by selection, it was possible to transfer the sex determining mechanism from the original pair of sex chromosomes to a new pair, formerly autosomes, which then took on the function of sex determination from the first pair. This was possible because sex determination in the guppy is dependent on only a few genes and it was possible to accumulate sex influencing genes on the second pair of chromosomes sufficient to over-shadow the sex determining potency of those of the original pair.

Winge and his colleagues were also able to show that coloration in the male guppy is a very complex affair. The female in the wild type has very little color, whereas the male is quite brightly colored both on the body and on his longer and differently shaped fins. Coloration in the wild guppy is thus sex limited. The majority of genes affecting color are carried both by the male and the female. Only in the male, however, are these genes normally allowed expression, so that the color latent in the female is not determinable without modern techniques such as hormone treatment. Other color genes are transmitted only from male to male and these, of course, are visible in the male fish so that his contribution to his potential offspring is known.

Myron Gordon, who was the author of an earlier TFH book on the keeping of guppies, was an outstanding student of, and authority on, the live-bearing fishes. He himself worked out further details on inheritance in the guppy although his greatest contributions were perhaps to our knowledge of some of the other live-bearing fishes. Gordon at one stage kept about 600 tanks of different live-bearers, encompassing a great range of wild fresh-water and domestic types, from which his studies of inheritance in these fishes were made. The amateur fancier certainly does not require an aquarium set-up of this magnitude for his work but as we shall see later, it is, in fact, necessary to maintain a rather large number of tanks if there is to be a serious program of breeding of the live-bearing fishes.

Before his death in July 1969, Paul Hahnel, here photo-graphed at work by M. F. Roberts, was probably the most widely-known guppy breeder.

1. MAINTENANCE

Most authorities are in agreement that for the development of the usual strains of guppies, it is preferable to use medium sized tanks about 10 to 20 gallons in capacity. Too small a tank inhibits the growth of the fishes, but too large a tank not only limits the capacity of the normal aquarist to fit as many tanks as are necessary into the space available, but also wastes breeding capacity. The guppy is a small fish and small groups of breeders do not need more than 20 gallons or so for the full development of their young. The guppy breeds within the temperature range of about 68 to 80°F, having a somewhat shorter period of gestation at the higher temperature. In nature, reproduction is seasonal and the fishes have a resting period during the cooler months of the year, but this is not necessary, and it is the custom of breeders to continue the breeding throughout the whole year by maintaining uniform water temperature.

There need be nothing particularly fancy about the tanks and it is not necessary for them to be planted, but the aquarist may choose to have a nice-looking display of planted tanks which do have the advantage not only of decoration but also that the plants assist in keeping the water pure by absorbing waste material as they grow. However, plants need an adequate layer of sand in the tank and they need appropriate lighting in order to flourish and their addition to the breeding set-up necessarily thus involves more work and more expensive equipment than is otherwise necessary. The water can be kept sufficiently pure and aerated by filtration, or even by aeration alone if sufficient changes of water are made at regular intervals. In bare tanks it is also much easier than in planted tanks to get the fishes out.

Hahnel's famous giant guppies photographed against water sprite (*Cera-topteris thalictroides*) by Mervin F. Roberts.

If the tanks are kept together in a breeding room, it is very much easier to heat the room when necessary than to heat each tank individually. However, if this is inconvenient or impracticable, the easiest form of heating is nowadays provided by a combined thermostat and heater to be placed in each tank so that failure of any component affects only the particular tank concerned. Although it is possible to control a whole bank of tanks by having a thermostat in only one of them controlling all of the heaters in the rest, it will be realized that a failure of this thermostat can result in the loss of fishes in all the tanks. Any thermostat-controlled heating device of the type mentioned should be adequate but not much more than adequate in heating capacity for this purpose. Probably more fishes are killed by being cooked due to thermostats sticking in closed position than are killed by being chilled because of a thermostat remaining open. If the heater is not of too high a wattage, the tank will not rise to a dangerous temperature even when the thermostat sticks in a closed position. A further safeguard may be added by having a second thermostat in series with the first, perhaps set at a somewhat higher temperature. If the first fails to open, the second should do so as the temperature rises.

The more guppies one attempts to keep per gallon of water, the more necessary it will be to aerate or both to aerate and filter the tanks. If aeration alone is used and is giving a spray of fine bubbles, this should be adequate. Filtration alone may be used without additional aeration since the act of filtration aerates the water to a considerable extent. Only if the fishes are really crowded, which should not occur, will it be absolutely necessary to use both aeration and filtration. The filter is needed to remove gross particles from the water and this is achieved by filtering through materials such as finely spun glass wool, dacron wool, or even fine-grained sand. A layer of finely divided activated charcoal added to the filter will take up a great deal of very fine particles and dissolved unwanted chemical materials from the water, including even obnoxious gases. If the charcoal is fairly coarsely divided, i.e. with grain size up to $\frac{1}{4}$-inch, quite a considerable amount will be needed. If, however, really finely divided charcoal is used of more like pinhead size, a layer of one or 2 ounces will service a 20 gallon tank for two or three months. In addition, the use of such finely divided charcoal does not carry with it as much danger of upsetting tank conditions as does that of larger amounts of a coarser charcoal. This is because there is always the danger of the gradual leaching of contaminants from the charcoal to the water, which can be avoided by washing fine grain charcoal beforehand, but which is not so easily done with the coarser-grained material. This is why magazine articles tend to warn against immediately using a filter-capacity amount of charcoal in an aquarium, and advise adding it very slowly bit by bit to the filter or turning the filter on only for very short periods initially. If washed fine-grained charcoal is used it can be placed into the filter, which can then be turned on and immediately left running fully.

The undergravel filter is very efficient both as an oxygenator and for keeping tanks sparkling clear. It may be used alone or in a planted tank but of course needs gravel at the bottom of the tank. Its only drawbacks are that it tends to rob plants of their nutriment and should therefore be turned on only for part of the day, and when a bare tank contains an undergravel filter this must eventually be cleaned out since the gravel at the bottom becomes gradually clogged by waste material which has to be eliminated. In a small bare tank, this is no real problem, and the undergravel filter may be highly commended for use in such circumstances.

It has been mentioned that guppies should be kept at 68 to 80°F. They can tolerate anywhere between 65° and 85° but they will not breed reliably at the bottom of that range. For breeding, a temperature between 75° and 80° is best and the young themselves do best at about 80° for the first few weeks of life, after which the temperature may be lowered towards 75°. Some precautions should be taken as in any tropical aquarium to avoid rapid changes in temperature. Although a fish may be happy at 85° and equally happy at 65°, it will be very unhappy if the temperature is dropped from one to the other. It will then exhibit symptoms of chilling and will probably become diseased and die. Even an upward change of such a magnitude is quite undesirable and the fish may show signs of shock and heat exhaustion.

All changes in water temperature should therefore be quite gradual; a downward change should not exceed 2 or 3°F and an upward change should not normally exceed 5°F. There is one exception: if newly arrived fishes have been thoroughly chilled, it has usually been found better to raise the temperature quite rapidly to within the normal range than to keep them at too low a temperature for any longer period. When rather small tanks are used, there is always the danger of an undetected swing in temperature overnight. Such a swing of perhaps 6° to 8° is sometimes found to explain poor health in the fishes and apparently inexplicable outbreaks of disease.

When there is a really hot spell and severe danger of the tanks rising in temperature to above 90°, it may be necessary to take precautions. These should take the form of draping wet, thick cloth over the tanks so as to cool them as far as possible by evaporation. It may even be necessary to place cubes of ice in the tanks to help cool the water. The fishes will avoid contact with the ice and there need be no worry about their becoming chilled from such a source. With an insulated fish room this problem will not normally arise and it will not usually arise with large tanks. We, however, are discussing medium-sized aquaria in which water temperature may rise rather rapidly with the outside temperature. The above precautions, together with turning up the aerator somewhat should in all normal circumstances be sufficient to carry the fishes through a heat wave.

Thick plantings such as shown in the Ruda Zukal photo enable fry to evade their cannibalistic elders.

2. WATER QUALITY

There are various aspects of water quality which must be considered when dealing with any tropical fishes. These include pH, the hardness, and the salinity of the water. Guppies can stand very considerable variations in each of these different factors; but, as with water temperature, the change from one level of pH, hardness, or salinity to another should not be abrupt. As we shall see later, guppies are thought to do best in somewhat acid water and water which is on the hard rather than the soft side. Also they like a fair degree of salinity and as we have already seen can actually flourish in marine water. Each of the factors mentioned should be measured so that the hobbyist is aware of the water conditions in which his fishes are living. After measurement it may be necessary to correct one or more of them. Methods will be described by which this can be accomplished.

Measuring and Adjusting pH

Most of us will be familiar with the measurement of pH. There are various ways of doing it, but the simplest method involves only a determination of the acidity or alkalinity of the water with a suitable color change indicator; less accurately with papers impregnated with such an indicator that may be dipped in to the aquarium water. A suitable measure of pH can be obtained by adding to 10 c.c. of tank water (about 2 teaspoons) one half of a c.c. of indicator solution, which is about 10 drops, containing 0.1% bromothymol blue. The color which results should be compared with those on a chart or it can be placed into a so-called color comparator, which can be purchased from dealers or from pharmacists. With the comparator, the color developed can be more accurately compared with the standard colors than just by a chart alone. When the water is acid, there will be a yellow color; when it is around neutral, the color will be greenish, and when it is alkaline, the color changes to blue. The total range of pH with bromothymol blue is from 6.0 to approximately 7.6. After a certain amount of practice, the aquarist may be so accustomed to the appearance of these different colors that he can dispense for approximate measurements at least with any actual color comparisons.

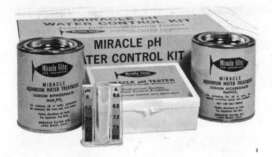

Your local petshop has various types of water control kits to measure and adjust pH.

The pH of the tank can be adjusted by the addition of acid or alkaline sodium phosphate or on the alkaline side alone by the addition of sodium bicarbonate. A suitable mixture of phosphates gives a so-called buffered solution which is resistant to changes in pH for as long as the chemicals in it remain intact. It is therefore preferable to use the phosphates to bicarbonate even when adjusting only on the alkaline side. However, the point is not of great importance because the aquarium will gradually change in pH despite the buffering if the circumstances are such as to cause excessive acidification or too strong an alkaline condition.

To change the pH of the tank of water, obtain 1% solutions of the two phosphates as indicated above and then take a measured quantity of water from the tank, say 1 pint, and slowly add small quantities of whichever phosphate is needed, testing at intervals until the correct pH is obtained. Having measured the amount required to bring a pint of the tank water to the correct pH, multiply by the number of pints in the aquarium and add slowly the necessary amount of phosphate to the water. Bear in mind that the pH of a tank should never be changed too much at one time or the fishes will suffer. When the tank is at the desired pH, the whole maneuver may be completed by adding a buffered mixture of the phosphates to the tank as indicated above so that the new pH shall be maintained as long as possible. Add about 10 c.c., (two teaspoons) of this mixture of 1% solutions per gallon of water to the aquarium. Incidentally, although we are dealing with pH first in this text, it is wise to adjust the pH of the tank after making all the other adjustments that may be needed.

There has been a considerable comment, particularly when dealing with breeding killie fish and other surface minnows, about adjusting the pH of water on the acid side by means of a peat filter. It is asserted that the acid pH so produced is in some way more natural and that in consequence, the fishes do better and that the eggs and fry stand a better chance of survival. This has not been fully proved but it should not be practiced for guppies. Although they do better in acid water, it is not acid soft water that they require, and this is what will be produced by the use of peat or similar organic filters.

Measuring and Adjusting Hardness
Another water quality that should be measured is the hardness. This is not nearly as often measured as it should be, and the adjustment of it becomes more and

more essential as we try to achieve perfection in fish breeding. There are several types of outfit available which may be obtained from your dealer, many of which appear to give a satisfactory and sufficiently accurate measurement. Hardness can even be measured electrometrically, but this is not really necessary. A preferred method is the versenate technique. Hardness is usually expressed in parts per million (p.p.m.) of calcium carbonate, or in so-called degrees of hardness in Germany. One German degree of hardness equals approximately 18 p.p.m. Soft water is rather arbitrarily defined as having less than about 100 parts per million hardness and hard water may contain up to several hundred parts per million. Very soft water has almost none at all. Hardness is not necessarily caused by calcium alone and may be contributed to by magnesium and certain other elements. It is

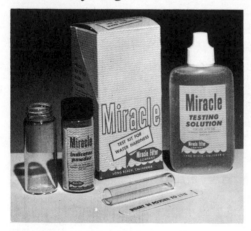

Water hardness test kits can be found at most aquarium shops.

measured with calcium, however, as though it were that element. If necessary, it can be measured quite separately in a modification of the versenate method but there is not usually any need to do this. Soft water is usually acid to neutral and hard water is usually alkaline. However, this is not necessarily so, and it is easy to manufacture artificial waters which are hard and acid, or soft and alkaline.

Adjusting the hardness of aquarium water may be done in at least two ways. If it is too soft, it is quite easy to add more calcium, usually in the form of calcium chloride, to bring it up to the required degree of hardness. If it is too hard, it is possible to soften the water by an appropriate ion-exchange resin filter, or part of the water can be discarded and replaced by pure distilled water or clean rain water to an extent indicated by the amount of softening required. Water softening pillows can be obtained from dealers. They usually contain ion-exchange resins but they are fairly slow in action. It is best to buy resin in granular form from your dealer or from a pharmacist and to add it as part of the filter bed so that a fairly rapid action may be obtained. Use the sodium form of the resin, which will exchange hard elements in the water for sodium chloride; of course, salinity will thereby be increased. If this is not desired, the hydrogen form can be used when hydrogen chloride (hydrochloric acid) will be released into the water as the hard material is absorbed, and it will then have to be corrected for pH.

If necessary, a mixture of resins can be purchased which will remove everything and give virtually distilled water. It will not, of course, be sterile. Such a resin is Zeocarb 225 made by the Permutit Company of England. This will soften 100 or 200 gallons of water per pound of resin, depending on the hardness originally present, and the resin may be reactivated by a simple chemical procedure. But hardening soft water is very easy. Simply add the required amount of calcium chloride to the tank. If your tank has a hardness of 50 parts per million as calcium and you want to have 200 parts per million, then 150 parts per million must be added. This is 150mg. of calcium per litre or approximately 9 grains per gallon as calcium or about 25 grains per gallon as calcium chloride in the anhydrous form. It is hardly ever necessary to harden water by adding magnesium as well as or instead of calcium, so this aspect will be neglected.

Measuring and Adjusting Salinity

We are concerned also with the measurement of salinity. It is both important and easy to measure and yet it is very rarely done. Probably the simplest way is to titrate the aquarium water against silver nitrate using potassium chromate as an indicator. Silver nitrate is soluble in water but when it comes in contact with sodium chloride, a precipitate of the almost insoluble silver chloride appears. The silver nitrate will exchange to silver chloride preferentially as long as there is sodium chloride present for it to act upon. However, when all of the sodium chloride that constitutes the salinity of the water has been used up by the silver nitrate, it will then exchange for the chromate present as an indicator and give a bright red precipitate of silver chromate. Therefore, as soon as one sees red appearing in the water being titrated, that is the end of the titration and the amount of silver nitrate which has been used gives an estimate of the salinity of the aquarium water. Any pharmacist can tell you how to make up appropriate solutions and how to use them. Typical tap water will contain about 50 parts per million (0.005%) of salinity. Aquarium water often builds up a salt content of ten times this or 500 parts per million. This, of course, particularly occurs when salt has been purposely added. If this level is much exceeded, plants are likely to suffer. Some of them are affected by more than 300 or 400 parts per million. Marine water is very salty and contains up to 3% of sodium chloride. This is 30,000 parts per million and very much higher than would normally be encountered in the fresh water aquarium.

Adjusting salinity resembles adjusting for hardness. Water which is too salty may be diluted with pure water or it may be desalted with ion-exchange resin. If the latter is done, it is best done with the combination of resins mentioned above, either mixed into a single filter or kept separate. The advantage of keeping them separate is that each can then be regenerated and used again. It will more frequently be necessary to increase the salinity when guppies are being kept. This is best done by adding the necessary amount of pure sodium chloride. So-called rock salt or butcher's salt may be used in place of the pure article but do not use table salt, which will give a cloudy solution, because it contains materials added to prevent agglutinating in moist conditions. Remember that one level teaspoon per gallon increases salinity by about 1,000 parts per million or 0.1%. This is far more than is needed for most purposes.

The addition of sea water is not usually desirable. A mixture of sea water and fresh water is called brackish and it contains many minerals other than sodium chloride. It is both hard and alkaline at the same time. If we wish, we could start with pure, distilled water at the beginning and could omit all measurements of pH, hardness, etc., and just add suitable chemicals to the distilled water. For instance, ten gallons of distilled water to which are added 5 level teaspoons of rock salt and 100 c.c. of an equal mixture of sodium mono- and dihydrogen phosphates will be of practically zero hardness, 500 parts per million salinity, and pH 6.8.

Only after we have made measurements of pH, hardness, and salinity do we know enough about the water in a tank to use it intelligently or to modify it. There are many other measurements we could make, such as the amount of nitrogen or organic matter in the water as an index of its purity, or we could measure the amount of dissolved gases as an index of the capacity of the water to support life. These may be important on special occasions, but the measurement of pH, hardness, and salinity is frequently important and is almost always needed for sustained success in the breeding of many species of fishes. Always remember, with fishes living in a tank, to make any changes gradually and carefully so that the inhabitants are not disturbed or injured. If the tank is empty, sudden and complete changes can be made in preparation for the fishes which it may eventually contain. Many tanks show day to night changes in pH which are not harmful as long as the swing is not extreme.

Unnecessarily fine distinctions have been made by some writers about the pH in which guppies should be kept. Some advocate different levels for different colored guppies, such as 6.5 to 6.8 for reds, and 6.8 to 7.0 for blues, but this is generally speaking quite unreasonable and a pH of between 6.5 and 7.0 is usually satisfactory for any type of guppy. Using the standards discussed above, the best water for guppies in the opinion of the majority of breeders will have about 500 to 1,000 (not more) parts per million salinity, and will be of medium hardness. This is a hardness of about 6 to 10 degrees on the German scale or about 100 to 180 parts per million. If plants are to be kept in the tanks with the fish, keep the salinity and the hardness down to and certainly not higher than this. Salinity will not usually be changed by the presence of plants, but the hardness of the water and its pH may gradually change when they are present. This, and the occasional partial changes of water which are desirable in any fish tank will mean that regular checks should be kept on the actual condition of the tanks from time to time, so purchase kits for the measurement of salinity, hardness, and pH, particularly the last two.

3. REPRODUCTION IN GUPPIES

It was realized early in the 18th century that some of the smaller fishes of the New World are viviparous, that is, they give birth to living young. It has taken a long time to disentangle the facts, and there is a great deal still to know. However, we now realize that these fishes actually nourish their young for a short period until they are born. The ovum does not leave the ovary as it does in the case of mammals. It stays within the ovarian follicle, that is, the crypt in the ovary where it has been developed. Sperm-atozoa penetrate up to the ovary during fertilization and impregnate the ova inside the follicles. Then, a kind of placenta similar in function to the placenta of mammals is developed but it is developed between the pericardium, the membrane surrounding the heart of the young embryo, and the wall of the ovarian follicle. This may seem very bizarre to those who have only studied the details of mam-malian biology, but in fact, the pericardial placenta per-forms the same functions of absorbing nourishment from the bloodstream of the mother as does the chorionic placenta of the mammal. Later, the young are freed from the ovary and travel down the female genital tract, the oviduct, and are eventually expelled. Despite all this, they still have a yolk sac, the bag containing the nourishment which was present in the egg when fertilization took place, and even after the young are released into the water, they subsist briefly upon the food stored within it. The young fishes develop in a folded position, head to tail, and are ejected with this fold still present. At birth they may sink to the bottom for a short period but they are usually able to look after themselves quite rapidly.

Six photographs by Milan Chvojka depict a female guppy ejecting her fry. They usually emerge in curled-up position and generally several appear in quick succession.

Fry may uncurl almost immediately, but often they sink to the bottom and remain there for several minutes before becoming active.

Whether becoming at once free-swimming or remaining temporarily balled-up on the substrate, fry soon set out in search of food.

The live-bearing fishes are the easiest of all fishes to breed. The only problem usually encountered is that of saving the young from the cannibalism of their parents. In natural circumstances, reproduction is seasonal but they will breed all the year around within a temperature range of about 68° to 80°F. There is no difficulty about telling

Ruda Zukal's photo might well be captioned: "How does he get two girl-friends?" Males at left are confronting the females to perform their courting dance; the one at right comes to join in the ritual or, as very often happens, the females have already spurned his suggestive display.

sex in even fairly young fishes. The male possesses a gonopodium, which is an organ of copulation formed from the modified anal fin. In addition, in the guppy, the males are normally brightly colored and the females are a dull grey or bluish color, although in some more recently developed strains, females also sometimes show quite bright coloration, particularly in their fins. There is a large difference in size between males and females in the various species of live-bearers, and this is certainly seen in the guppy. The fully adult male is perhaps no more than a fifth or a tenth of the weight of the fully developed female and he is correspondingly much thinner and smaller. He makes up for this by having bright coloration and varying degrees of flowing finnage including tail fins, which may in some of the more recently developed strains be extremely beautiful.

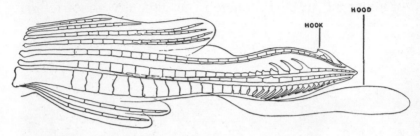

HOOK   HOOD

The drawing indicates the intricate composition of the gonopodium of a male guppy.

The disparity in size between mature female and male guppies is seen in this Helmut Pinter photo.

M. F. Roberts photo of Alger's blue-tailed males performing their quivering courtship dance while the female shows customary unconcern.

Courtship

The male guppy practices quite an elaborate courtship. This may be observed with males and females kept together, when the males are normally active most of the time in courting and chasing after the females. They swim beside the females in a path more or less parallel with them, then they may dart ahead and confront the female head on with the body curved and tail fins and pectoral fins quivering and held firmly out from the body. The female will often respond to this by curving her own body in an S-shape, which may be the position a pair may assume just prior to mating. Sometimes in addition to curving his body, the male may fold his dorsal and tail fins and again stand in the water in front of the female. Interspersed with the above maneuvers will be movements of the gonopodium. The resting position of the gonopodium is parallel to the body and pointing backwards, but it may be swung down or forwards or from side to side quite readily. Normally, the gonopodium will be swung sideways and upwards into a forward position and the pelvic fin on the same side as that to which the gonopodium has swung, will also move forward and more or less lock in with the gonopodium. The rays of the fin slip over each other and form with the gonopodium a tube through which packets of spermatozoa are ejected. The gonopodium in any one guppy may be swung just as frequently to the left side as the right side and the corresponding pelvic fin joins it on each occasion. These gonopodial movements may be seen to take place with or without the presence of the female but they are more frequent in her presence. When the female is present, the male will thrust the tip of the gonopodium towards her genital region. There may be single, rapid thrusts or there may be whole series of gonopodial movements and many times the female is not actually touched. This led some of the earlier authors to conclude that the gonopodium acted more or less like a pea shooter and that the packets of spermatozoa which are freed at this period were shot towards the right area of the female without the male actually coming into contact with her. Later investigations have shown that this isn't true and that, in fact, insemination only takes place if the tip of the gonopodium is actually inserted into or at least touches the female's urogenital region.

In numerous examinations following mating gestures, no spermatozoa have been found in the female's body unless the male gonopodium had been observed actually to touch the female in the urogenital area. Thus, the act of mating involves a definite contact between the gonopodium of the male and the genitalia of the female, but it only

American Museum of Natural History photos of pre-fertilization action:
extending the near pelvic fin and swinging the gonopodium down and forward
as he approaches the hovering female, the male is about ready, below, to make
contact with her genital pore.

lasts momentarily. Furthermore, it occurs rather infrequently in the course of the other courtship maneuvers that we have just been describing. During mating, there is therefore a physical locking of the gonopodium into the genitalia of the female which is aided by the spinous hooks which are on the tip of the gonopodium and make a lasting contact possible. The paired fish may even swim together in the aquarium for a short period and the act of copulation is terminated when they fall apart. Occasionally, the contact between the male and the female is difficult to break and may even occasion bleeding. In fact, cases have been described where breakage of contact failed and the male had actually died. As indicated above, the female has to co-operate in this to some extent. It used to be asserted that the female guppy was indifferent to the advances of the male but this isn't so, and she has to make definite movements, particularly a slow-moving circular swimming, otherwise the male cannot inseminate her.

Sex behavior in the guppy is conditioned by sex hormones. The testes of the male produces male hormone, probably testosterone, which not only causes his male development and coloration, but also causes his male sex behaviour. The corresponding, although milder sex behaviour of the female is also dependent upon her ovarian female hormones. It is to be presumed that the hormone concerned is estradiol as in the rest of the known vertebrates, but this is not certain. It is certain that both male and female guppies will respond to the corresponding mammalian hormones or to chemical substances made synthetically which have the same general properties. We shall see in a later section how the male hormone may actually be used upon the female to detect the color genes that she carries.

Fertilization and Growth of Unborn Young

Young live-bearing females can be fertilized at a very early stage of development, in the case of platys, at eight days of age or soon thereafter. Thus if kept together with mature males, the young live-bearers may be fertilized far too early for future health, and also not by males of the breeder's choice. However, if they are removed from the adults, it takes some time before the young males in any particular brood grow old enough to fertilize their sisters. Strangely, even when they have been fertilized quite early, the females do not bear young for many weeks and may be expected to drop their first brood not earlier than 10 to 12 weeks of age. Even then, they will have to be kept rather warm (about 78 to 80°F.) for it to occur this early. The sperm are stored in the female and may fertilize successive crops of egg cells for up to a period exceeding 6 months. If matings continue to occur, as of course they do in a tank of mixed males and females, the new sperm will fertilize a proportion of the eggs. How long the older

Arend van den Nieuwenhuizen photo of guppy embryos in a late stage of development.

sperm deposited by earlier fertilizations remain active enough not to be entirely superseded by newer sperm has not yet been determined.

Clearly, the first breeding of the female guppy is extremely important because it will determine the type of young she will produce for more than the litter which immediately follows. In the guppy (also in platys and swordtails and some other species of live-bearers) successive crops of eggs are fertilized at intervals so that one lot of young, all of the same age, is produced and is then followed about a month later by another batch. At an average temperature of 75°F., the time of development of the guppy from fertilization of the ovum to ejection of the fry is about 24 days, but the brood interval, that is, the actual time elapsing between the dropping of successive lots of young, is about 30 days. The extra time is taken up by the development of the next crop of eggs in the ovary of the female to the point of maturity for fertilization. In some other species of live-bearers (as in *Heterandria*), the eggs ripen and are fertilized much more at random, small batches of young being produced every few days and there is therefore always a continuous set of young at different stages of development present in the mother.

The cooler the water, the longer the guppy takes to produce its young. At about 80°F, and in a bright light, the young are produced at about 28 day intervals. At 68°F, still only if kept in a bright light, this interval lengthens to 35 or even 40 days. Below about 68°F, the interval lengthens indefinitely and few or no broods are produced. In a dull light, the brood interval also lengthens and cool conditions, together with dullness of illumination, will more rapidly produce cessation of breeding.

At birth, the young with the fold still present, sink to the bottom for a short period, but usually swim up into the water again quite rapidly. They are quite variable in size according to the age of the mother and the number of their brothers and sisters. The first brood from a young mother may not necessarily be particularly small, as she may only produce half a dozen to a dozen young and they will therefore be quite large. Later on, she may produce 60 or 80 young, even up to 100 or 200 in exceptional circumstances, and these will tend to be smaller than were the earlier ones because they are packed very tightly into the available space within the mother's body. The pregnant mother swells noticeably and also presents the well-known gravid spot, which is a dark area near the base of the anal fin and is caused by the stretching of the body tissues sufficiently to reveal the dark coloration of the peritoneal wall.

Saving the Young

Soon after being expelled into the water, the young swim up towards the light, a phenomenon known as positive phototropism. If the tank is heavily stocked with fine-leafed plants, particularly towards the lightest area of the tank, they will migrate into them and will be fairly safe from the adults; otherwise they are very likely to be eaten by them, and steps must be taken to prevent this from happening. For this reason, it has become the custom to use breeding traps in which the female is confined so that the young may escape before being eaten. The oldest form of such a trap is a funnel placed in the water with its lower aperture downwards so that the female is confined within the funnel itself but the young can escape by swimming down and out of the funnel mouth. This is by no means a good idea. First, it isn't very effective, and secondly, the mother should not be confined in so small a space. Various other traps are on the market or can be made by the fancier. The best are quite roomy, perhaps of half-gallon size, and allow the water in the tank to flow freely through them. They

Fancy guppies: Frank Alger's on opposite page as photographed by Dr.
Herbert R. Axelrod, and Paul Hahnel's in the M. F. Roberts photo above.

37

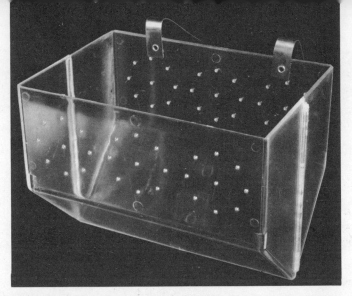

Aquarium shops have various types of "guppy traps" and net breeding traps to save your guppy babies. These same net traps can be used to isolate various strains of guppies in the same aquarium. It's almost like having an extra few tanks around.

can be made of glass rods strung together with nylon thread, or of netting spread over a frame so that the young can escape but the female is confined.

A well-fed mother generally does not eat her young; but just in case, it is advisable to take precautions. Great care should be taken about moving the female during advanced stages of pregnancy, otherwise she may be damaged or, even if not damaged, she may prematurely expel her young. Perhaps the most satisfactory of all breeding traps is a screen of mosquito or similar netting on a rustless frame which can be wedged across the tank so as to confine the female to one end of the tank while allowing the young to pass to the other end. In spite of all these methods, many breeders prefer the natural method of providing plenty of plant cover. The best plants for this purpose are masses of *Myriophyllum, Ambulia, Utricularia,* and *Nitella* or other filamentous algae. They are not too closely matted to prevent the young live-bearers from diving into the cover but are usually far too thick for the adults to follow and consume the young. Once the mother has dropped her brood she may be removed; this will not harm her and it is much better to move her than to attempt to catch and remove the young.

Some persons claim to be able to sex the young guppy immediately. Even if true, it is unnecessary; they may be left together until three or four weeks when it is quite easy to tell their sex. Then they may be separated and batches of males and females may be raised separately. The 10-gallon tank that we have advocated as being standard equipment for the breeding and raising of guppies will be adequate for the first month, then if the young are separated by sex, each group can be accommodated in a 10-gallon tank for the next month or two. Eventually, the guppies will be separated out into smaller, adult communities for the purpose of breeding. Correct feeding of the young guppies during this early period is extremely important and is discussed in a later section.

Female guppy gulping one of her fry; even well-fed fish instinctively snap up small moving organisms and some of the fry usually become victims.
M. F. Roberts photo

Reinhold Kleiss strain of guppies photographed by Dr. Herbert R. Axelrod.

4. FEEDING GUPPIES

In spite of a good deal of work that has been done, particularly by commercial firms, on the preparation of foods for fishes, we know surprisingly little about their actual food requirements. We are not even sure which

At the 1964 shows in Europe this type of "German Black" guppy with a red tail was winning prizes. Today this type of guppy is almost commonplace and is being raised in huge quantities, especially in Singapore. Photo by Hansen at the Berlin Aquarium.

of the known vitamins are necessary for fishes, or whether there are other vitamins which are not necessary for us but which are necessary for fishes. We know little about their detailed calorific requirements, about their need for a balance of protein, carbohydrate, fat, or of vegetable and animal matter, except in a very general way. Some fishes are known to feed almost entirely carnivorously, some almost entirely herbivorously, but others presumably take a mixture of the two. It is not surprising, therefore, that there are many ideas about the best food for guppies, almost as many ideas as there are persons who are serious keepers of guppies. What happens in the end is that we state that a variety of food should be taken, including as much as possible in the way of live food or freeze-dried foods. Thus we avoid concentrating on any single food which may prove to be insufficient, and we try to assure that the fishes obtain a mixture of all the different feasible constituents that they may need in their diet.

Preparation of Food

We should use as much live food as is possible but we should never use entirely live food for the simple reason that fishes can become accustomed to it and will not take prepared food or dried food when this is necessary. Sooner or later, we have to give fishes dried food because live food is unobtainable, and it is extremely disconcerting if they will not accept it. It is best, therefore, to feed a variety of food including live food such a brine shrimp, *Daphnia, Tubifex,* mosquito larvae, chopped up earth worms, and a variety of tinned or dried food such as chopped crab, fish meat, liver, and beef, to which is added vegetable components and one or two varieties of a good, commercially prepared dried, flaked, or pelleted food. Some fanciers avoid giving guppies any vegetable material but most of us feel that it is safer to

A patented process for freeze-drying fish foods has saved the guppy breeder quite a bit of work. Not only does Gordon's Formula come freeze-dried (so it sticks on the side of the aquarium glass and you can see how much has been eaten), but brine shrimp, tubifex, mosquito larvae and daphnia are also available. Freeze-drying preserves much of the taste, nutritional value, color and shape of the food while sterilizing it against harmful organisms.

include some of it. If we keep many guppies, it could be expensive to feed them with much commercially prepared food. In this instance, we may prefer to use our own home-made foods, and Gordon's formula which is given below is a very useful all-purpose food suitable for feeding any but the youngest fish. It has the advantage that it will keep fresh for quite some time without fouling the water and it can be nibbled by the guppies at the bottom of the tank.

The formula is:

> 1 pound of fresh beef liver,
> 20 tablespoons of Pablum or Ceravim,
> 2 teaspoons of table salt.

The apparatus needed for the preparation of Gordon's formula is a food blender which can be used for breaking up the food into a fine mash. The liver is skinned of its connective tissue covering, the larger blood vessels, and other tough or fibrous material are removed. It is then cut into approximately half inch cubes. Two ounces each of cubed liver and cold water are placed in the blender and beaten until they are liquid. This liquid liver solution is then strained into a bowl and the exercise is repeated until all of the liver has been passed through the blender and is liquidised and strained. The two teaspoons full of table salt are then added.

The Pablum of similar dry pre-cooked cereal is then stirred into it until a thick, peanut butter-like consistency is obtained. This is put into one-to four-ounce glass containers, the size depending on the amount used for a single day's feeding of the paste. The filled glass jars are placed in water and heated until the water boils. The heat is then turned off and the jars are allowed to stand in the hot water for about half an hour. Then they are allowed to cool and the glass containers are covered or capped in some way and kept in a deep-freeze. It is necessary to heat the liver mixture to coagulate the liquid elements of the liver. If this heat were not applied, the liver would separate out from the paste and would foul the water because it would still be partly in a fluid condition. In ordinary feeding, a portion of the liver paste varying in size according to need is placed in the tank and left for the fishes to nibble.

An attractively marked and variously colored double swordtail guppy. Photo by Hilmar Hansen, Aquarium Berlin.

Gordon used to feed his fishes only once a day, early in the morning so that they had the whole day to finish the portion of liver paste which had been given to them.

Any food remaining uneaten on the following morning was removed and replaced by a new feeding. However, the uneaten food if prepared according to the formula above remains intact and does not start fouling the tank unless it is left for more than one or two days. Gordon used to alternate this particular food with ordinary, pure dry shredded shrimp or live foods such as *Tubifex*, *Daphnia* or whiteworms. You can no doubt concoct variations of your own, adding shrimp or other materials to the liver paste if you wish. Commercial preparations of the famous Gordon formula are available at pet shops.

If guppies are not fed with a paste such as Gordon's, they must be fed quite frequently. The guppy cannot eat sufficient bulk to last more than an hour or two, and he must go on eating throughout the day or he will be undernourished. Therefore, it is not good to follow

Americans have led European aquarists in development of extensive tail finnage. Photo by Hilmar Hansen, Aquarium Berlin.

the rule as given in such good books as the one by Innes, to feed only as much as the fishes will consume during five minutes. This is all right if you feed every two or three hours, but it is not all right if the fishes are only fed twice daily. Many live foods, such as *Tubifex, Daphnia,* and mosquito larvae remain alive in the water until they are eaten and, like the liver paste, are quite safe to leave. If there is gravel in the tank, it is, however, rather dangerous to put too many *Tubifex* in because the worms will establish themselves at the bottom of the tank and can eventually foul the water. They should be placed in a feeder or a vessel from which they drop one by one into the water or are pulled out to be eaten by the fishes. Freeze-dried *Tubifex* can be stuck onto the side of the aquarium and will remain in a good, eatable condition until the fishes have finished it.

Thus, if the food used is not such as can be left in the tank, feeding should be virtually as frequent as possible, at least four to six times a day. Even ten times a day is not too frequent, particularly with younger fishes, but this is quite clearly not possible for many of us. However, if guppies are not able to eat fairly continuously, they will not develop to the best advantage. They will remain relatively stunted and they will not become the fine show fishes that most of us desire to produce. The fancier who wishes to feed live food must feed to excess so that uneaten food animals are always available in the tank or he must feed several times during the daytime. If he is forced into using dried food continuously, this food cannot be fed in sufficient quantities to last for more than one feeding or it will start fouling the tank, and he must feed his fishes several times a day or use some kind of automatic feeder. What he must not do is to depend on a morning and evening feeding to take care of his fishes. This is definitely insufficient. It is almost manifest that with the suggested frequent feeding, care must be taken to see that the tank is kept in a clean and pure condition.

Feeding the Young

The young guppy can eat within a few minutes after being ejected from the mother's body. It should be fed as frequently as the adult, but since it cannot eat a great variety of foods at first, the importance of two staple diets, newly-hatched brine shrimp and microworms, can hardly be exaggerated. Either of them, but preferably both, form a very good diet for the guppy during its first month or two of life. However, either alone can form an adequate food for the first few weeks. All the same, it is highly advisable to feed a variety of foods for the reasons stated above regarding adults, and it is therefore a good idea to commence feeding some finely-ground, dried foods to the young guppies within the first few days of life. This will also accustom them to it, and if it becomes necessary, they are able to be fed on it alone for a while.

It must be emphasized, as shown originally by Myron Gordon, that there is a tremendous difference between early, live-foods feeding and mixed or predominantly dried-food feeding in the guppy. The young guppy responds to live foods with a very much better growth rate and eventual development. Although it is possible to raise them on finely ground dried food even from the outset, this is therefore inadvisable and the result would be dwarf fish compared with those which are raised on

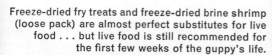
Freeze-dried fry treats and freeze-dried brine shrimp (loose pack) are almost perfect substitutes for live food ... but live food is still recommended for the first few weeks of the guppy's life.

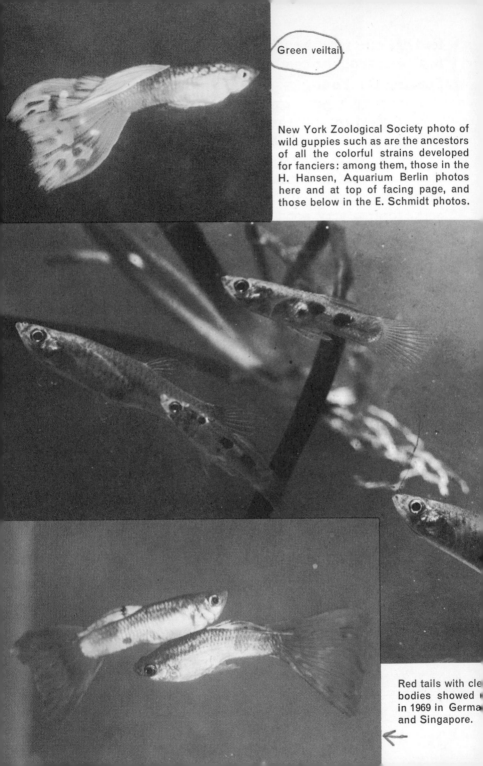

Green veiltail.

New York Zoological Society photo of wild guppies such as are the ancestors of all the colorful strains developed for fanciers: among them, those in the H. Hansen, Aquarium Berlin photos here and at top of facing page, and those below in the E. Schmidt photos.

Red tails with cle
bodies showed
in 1969 in Germa
and Singapore.

Dark blue fantail.

King Cobra fantail.

Half-black fantail.

live food. The brine shrimp, *Artemia salina*, is a crustacean and it is a live food of tremendous importance. As the reader probably knows, its eggs may be purchased commercially in very large numbers. These are dried and stored in vacuum packs and can be hatched out even years after they have been originally collected. There are two main types of brine shrimp available on the market. Culture and maintenance of the San Francisco brine shrimp has been understood for many years. The brine shrimp of the Great Salt Lake in Utah produce eggs somewhat larger than those of the San Francisco brine shrimp and they require a somewhat different hatching medium, as noted on packaging labels.

Both varieties may be raised either in shallow pans or in deep culture, in which case they need aeration. Deep culture is in bottles, (usually gallon jars or five gallon jars or carboys can be used for hatching) and several teaspoons of brine shrimp eggs per vessel yields quantities of the minute newly-hatched brine shrimp within a day or two of setting up the hatch. The eggs appear to be a fine, brown powder and are of no food value. Incubation occurs only in salt water, and they hatch more quickly and more evenly in weaker salt solutions than are needed for maintenance of the adults. Sea water is an excellent hatching medium for the San Francisco brine shrimp (not good for the Utah variety); to prepare a substitute, use six heaped tablespoonfuls of salt to each gallon of water, which gives about the same strength of salt solution as sea water. The eggs will float on the surface and should be sprinkled on the water and left there, using not more than one teaspoon of eggs per two gallons of water or in a deeper vessel, about twice that quantity if aeration is employed so that the eggs swirl around in the water. They will hatch in one to two days at a temperature of 70°F. and will take very much longer if they are kept at less than about 65°F. If too many eggs are used, many will not hatch out and the total hatch will be much the same as when fewer eggs are used. For Utah variety of brine shrimp, exactly the same procedures may be followed except that the solution required for hatching must have borax added at two teaspoonfuls per gallon.

If the eggs have been floated on the surface of shallow water, they will remain there and the newly-hatched shrimp can be siphoned off if care is taken not to disturb the water surface, while tipping the vessel gently so as to siphon off all possible shrimp. You will find it possible to leave only a teaspoon or two of water behind on which all of the empty egg shells have accumulated. The shrimp can be strained through a clean piece of cloth and washed with fresh water so as not to introduce unwanted salt to the aquarium. If the eggs have been swirled around in the water by the deep culture method, they must be allowed to settle out before siphoning off. Even then it is not quite so easy to get a clean separation between the shrimp and the eggs as is possible by the flotation method. Brine shrimp can be fed and grown to fair size or even to maturity. Indeed, it is possible to keep a culture of brine shrimp going so that samples can be taken and fed to the fishes at intervals. It isn't worth doing this normally, however, and we shall consider only the hatching and almost immediate utilization of the newly-hatched brine shrimp for the feeding of young fishes. Generally speaking, it will be more profitable to purchase adult brine shrimp, which are available in many areas in the live form, or to use deep-frozen brine shrimp instead of live ones for the feeding of larger fish.

The other food, microworms (*Anguillula silusiae*), is a small species of worm found in the soil. They were first cultivated by Swedish aquarists. This is a very interesting live-bearing worm attaining a maximum length of only about one tenth of an inch. It is, of course, very much smaller when young and is therefore an important food for young fishes. They are considerably cheaper to cultivate in large numbers than are brine

Dr. Eduard Schmidt tried to produce strains of guppies with crescents in their tails (see also bottom photo page 49), but he was unable to fix the strain.

shrimp but cultivation is somewhat more of a nuisance. The younger stages are smaller than newly hatched brine shrimp and may be useful when feeding particularly tiny fry. Guppy fry, however, can eat the adult microworms. The worm is easy to cultivate. It is kept in shallow vessels with tight covers, each vessel containing about a quarter of an inch of any of the quick-cooking breakfast oatmeals or wheatmeals, or even wheat-germ. The meal is cooked with milk, or water can be used, just as for ordinary use

Hilmar Hansen photographed this prize-winning fantail at the Berlin Aquarium in 1965.

but without adding salt. It is then inoculated with a little baker's yeast and, of course, with some microworms. In a few days, these will have formed a mass usually accumulating on the surface of the meal, but if small pieces of wet wood are criss-crossed over the meal so that the top ones are clear of it, the worms crawl up and collect on the top pieces. They will also crawl up the side of the vessel, particularly if it is roughened in some way. Sub-cultures can be made whenever needed from

When their tails are too large and their caudal peduncle is too delicate to properly carry the tail, the guppy swims awkwardly. This is called "deportment" in most guppy standards and this fish would have a very low deportment rating. Compare this fish to the two fish on the facing page. Note how strong their caudal peduncles appear and how straight they can carry their tails. Photo by Hilmar Hansen at the Berlin Aquarium.

existing ones and it is usually best to keep on sub-culturing rather than to try to feed existing cultures. Each one will last for two or three weeks and the worms do best at a rather warm temperature, up to about 75°F. The culture medium should be dampened occasionally as the microworm can't withstand desiccation. An equally important new white worm, somewhat larger than the microworm, but a good deal smaller than the original white worm, is called the Grindal worm and was introduced by Mrs. Morton Grindal, another Swedish aquarist. It is, at the most, half an inch in length and rather slimmer than the microworm. The adult Grindal worm is rather large for newly dropped guppies but the young worms are an excellent food for them.

The great advantage of using brine shrimp or microworms is that both will last in the aquarium for quite some time. Thus, they can be generously fed only once or twice a day and a sufficient number will be around for the young fishes to go on eating throughout the day. These foods and subsequent larger live foods, together with Gordon's mixture, can solve the problem of the relatively constant intake of food that is required by the young and the growing, and to a lesser extent by the adult guppy.

Some breeders keep the lights on over the tanks containing young fishes for a considerable period out of the 24 hours, some continuously. Nobody seems to have made any careful study of the effects of this type of prolonged feeding. All one can say is that prolonged lighting does not seem to harm the young fishes and that they do grow quicker when continually fed. One imagines that a compromise between virtually continuous lighting and the natural period of daylight in any particular locality is a good idea; it would be quite in order to keep the guppies illuminated, and therefore feeding, for about 16 or 18 hours each day.

If an appreciable amount of dried food is for some reason or another to be used, it is only necessary to make a mixture of a suitable grade of cereal and dried shrimp and to keep this in airtight containers so that it does not become a culture medium for mites or unwanted larvae. Such home-made foods are worth making if you wish to keep fish in quantity. They are much cheaper than marketed varieties and the user knows what is in them. It is quite unnecessary to manufacture pastes and to cook them and then grind them up again as often advocated by writers on the subject. It is only necessary to make preparations of this sort if Gordon's formula is to be used, which is quite a different type of fish food, adaptable to being gently nibbled away in the water. However, for someone who decides that he would like to make such a dried food of his own, Gordon, in another context, advocates the following:—

Liver of beef—5 lbs.
Pablum or Ceravin—14 lbs.
Shrimp shell meal—6 lbs.
Shredded shrimp meat—3 lbs.
Spinach—3 lbs.

We can see from the above that Gordon kept a large number of fishes. Use fractional measurements for a trial preparation.

The raw beef liver is cut into two-inch pieces and boiled for 15 minutes, then removed and the same water is used for boiling the other ingredients while the boiled liver is ground or chopped, and returned to the mixture for a further 15 minutes boiling. The resultant paste is then dried and ground for storage. The fineness of the grinding will determine the suitability of the particular ground-up food for different sizes of fish or their fry.

Paul Hahnel's strain of guppies photographed by Dr. Herbert R. Axelrod.

Hormone-treated female. Mutations among guppies are not rare and selection of sports for breeding has led to development of many strains. Zukal photo

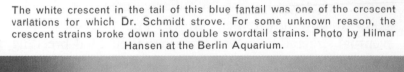

Dr. Eduard Schmidt (who later changed his name to Schmidt-Focke) developed this strain of top sword lace guppy. It is believed that this fish became the base for the King Cobra and the English Lace guppies.

The white crescent in the tail of this blue fantail was one of the crescent variations for which Dr. Schmidt strove. For some unknown reason, the crescent strains broke down into double swordtail strains. Photo by Hilmar Hansen at the Berlin Aquarium.

5. RAISING THE YOUNG

As the young fry grow, and at about a month of age, they may be separated according to sex. These can be then placed into different tanks so that they can be selected as desired for later matings. It is usually advisable to keep them in separate sex groups until the age of three to four months to attain as much size as possible before using them for breeding. Early breeding of females tends to slow down their growth and to reduce their eventual size and therefore to reduce their total breeding capacity. In addition, in any batch of guppies, some of the females will be used for show and these will usually be desired as large as possible. It is the same story with the males. It doesn't seriously matter how early a male is used for breeding but if he is used too early, his full development will not have been attained and it is not possible to tell whether he is of really first class potential. There should be absolutely no question of leaving males and females to breed together in a single batch. Everything will go wrong. First, they will breed at too early an age; secondly, the quicker, smaller, and more runt-like males will do most of the fertilizing. This will result in a rapid deterioration of the stock of guppies even though the strain had previously been brought to a relatively perfect state.

Some breeders have advocated the raising of the young fishes in pairs. Eventually, some of the couples will likely be found to be of the same sex. It is also difficult to raise small numbers of guppies successfully. Pairs in small containers are liable to be overfed and possibly not flourish and grow as well as they otherwise would. If they are in large containers, the overfeeding problem remains although it is not likely to cause such serious trouble in a larger tank, and large tanks for pairs entail a waste of space. All told, it is very much better to raise the young in groups by sex until one is ready to mate them and to select out the most desirable for mating.

There seems to be a very considerable variance between different strains of guppy in respect to the rate at which they grow and mature. Kaufman has described three main stages in the development of the fancy guppy. In body growth, about 70% of its eventual size should be attained at about four months; tail growth (which only starts in some strains at about the fourth month onwards) should reach maximum size at about seven months, growth of the dorsal fin occurs last of all and approximately during the period between seven and nine months. It is quite clear that this is not true of all strains of guppy, some of which attain excellent development of both tail and other finnage as early as four to six months of age. It will therefore be necessary for the fancier to become familiar with the characteristic growth stages of the particular strains of guppies with which he is dealing. Clearly, it is an advantage to have rapidly maturing fishes. These will go through more generations per year than is possible if one must wait nine or ten months to select the best fish. In some strains, it is quite clearly possible to make this selection well within six months. This particularly applies to selection of the male. Selection of the females, if they have been well and robustly fed, is possible at an even earlier age. Females can be bred at about four months if they have been properly raised and fed. This makes the most of their potential for the production of young as they will begin to decline in fertility after the age of eight or ten months.

It is best to breed the selected young guppies in small communities rather than in individual pairs or in larger communities. Several pairs, depending on the size of the tanks to be used but characteristically, four or five pairs in a ten gallon tank will form a useful breeding nucleus. This will avoid an undue degree of inbreeding and, at the same time, provide an opportunity for selecting only the very best of the fishes for continued breeding of the stock. We shall additionally, however, describe methods of more strict inbreeding in which brother-sister pairs, for example, may be maintained as in the strict inbreeding seen in experimental mouse colonies. This has certain advantages but only if the breeder can afford a great deal of care and a great deal of space and a great deal of time. Otherwise, the breeding in small communities is much to be preferred.

Dr. Herbert R. Axelrod photo of a Frank Alger male.

An early double swordtail, less colorful than strains later produced through discriminating crosses made by breeders. Photo by E. Schmidt.

Snakeskin pattern of the male and distinctive finnage of both sexes of an attractive guppy pair are photographed by M. F. Roberts.

61

6. KEEPING GUPPIES HEALTHY

Once a disease-free strain of guppies has been obtained and is kept in isolation, the only source of disease will be through the introduction of new fishes or of infected food or water. These should therefore be stringently guarded against. Any new fish should be placed in quarantine tanks for at least two weeks after they have been obtained and they should be observed very carefully during this period for the possible development of any signs of disease. They may even be treated prophylactically as though they have some of the commoner diseases in an attempt to prevent them from being carriers of unrecognised infections. Most fanciers, however, do not go to that extreme.

All live foods which have been obtained from outside should also be treated with considerable care. Do not collect *Daphnia*, mosquito larvae, and above all do not collect *Tubifex* worms, or get them from your dealer, and place them immediately into the fish tank. Make sure that they are thoroughly washed and cleaned before giving them to your fishes. Live foods such as newly-hatched brine shrimp or microworms which have been raised on the premises may be fed with considerably less caution. If any trouble does arise, remember to be clean in your habits. Do not handle infected materials and then start to service your fish tanks without thoroughly washing your hands first. Similarly, sterilize all nets, thermometers, and other implements that may be used first in one tank and then in another. Whipping into scalding water is the best way to assure sterility of nets.

In order to avoid outbreaks of disease all tanks should be scrutinized with a critical eye at frequent intervals; every day is not too often. Take note of how the fish are behaving; if they are not swimming naturally in the water with reasonably erect finnage and normal movements, suspect that something is wrong even though you cannot see any visible signs of disease. Fishes which are scrubbing themselves against rocks or plants, that have unnaturally drooped fins, that are swimming without progressing through the water at a normal speed, that are hugging the bottom or top of the aquarium, or that are abnormal in color should all be suspected of being sick. Apart from the question of behaviour, look also for direct signs of disease and parasitic organisms. These will naturally be visible only if they are infesting the surface of the fish, but many of the most commonly recognized ailments are of such a nature. Look for any raggedness of the fins, any discoloration of the fins or body, reddish streaks indicating hemorrhage, and patchy discoloration indicating areas of infestation. Look for the occurrence of small spots of any type, whether white or yellow in color, on the skin of the fish. Look at the eyes to assure that they are normal in appearance; note the rate at which gills are moving to see whether or not this is unusually fast. These physical signs are clues to the trouble from which the fish may be suffering.

It should be remembered that not all fishes showing abnormal behaviour are necessarily infected; their abnormal behaviour may be caused by some kind of toxin in the water, the commonest of which will be metal poisoning. Small amounts of copper, zinc, or cadmium in the water will poison fishes and cause distress, abnormalities of behavior, and of course susceptibility to diseases. Therefore, if you see abnormal behavior without visible signs indicating a particular infection, suspect that there may be water poisoning. Look for any

Dark blue triangles that won first place in their class at London show of 1969. Dr. Eduard Schmidt photo.

source of metallic contamination of the water; think back over what may have happened during the last few days. Take all precautions against any contact of metal and the aquarium water, other than metals such as stainless steel. If necessary, see what happens when you place one or two distressed fishes into otherwise suitable aquarium water from another source; if they recover within a few hours, poisoning of the original water should be strongly suspected and appropriate changes made as soon as possible.

The way to treat a sick fish depends very much upon the condition it is exhibiting and also on whether a single fish is affected in a tank of otherwise normal inhabitants, or whether a number or even all of the fish in a particular tank are showing signs of distress. In the first case, it is better to take out the sick fish and to attempt individual treatment, while of course keeping a careful eye on the course of events in the tank from which it has been removed. If many or all of the fishes in a tank appear to be affected, it is much more sensible procedure to treat the whole tank of fishes and not to wait for any further developments. A sick individual of no outstanding merit is best killed, but a sick fish which is

worth saving should of course be treated in a small tank or jar in which it can be isolated. Remember however that it is hard to keep a single isolated fish healthy and properly fed in a small tank; see that it is returned to a tank of normal dimensions as soon as this is feasible.

Remedies available for the treatment of fish diseases have become established over the course of many years. Some treatments suggested are little more than derivates from old wives' tales, whereas others are well established and effective. Curiously, the use of some of the most efficient modern drugs known to human clinical medicine is not always to be advocated in the fish tank. Antibiotics have their uses but they are not as widely useful as might be supposed and there are several reasons for this. First, antibiotics are still expensive and adequate dosage to any but the smallest tank of fishes can be rather prohibitive. Secondly, many of them tend to upset the balance of the aquarium water, rendering it colored or cloudy or otherwise unsuitable for inhabitation by the fishes. Most of the cures or remedies which are applied to the tropical fish tank are not particularly advanced ones; they represent the application of some well-known drugs or disinfectants, rather than the newer antiobiotic drugs. There is also the point that rather more fish diseases that are at present recognized and which we are capable of treating are caused by protozoa (which are minute animals) rather than by bacteria which are more readily attacked by antibiotics.

Aquarists have long been woefully ignorant of many fish diseases, particularly those which affect fishes internally. Now available in English, however, is Dr. Amlacher's book comprehensively covering the subject. Following are a few common diseases affecting the guppy, and some remarks about disease control in general.

White Spot

Ichthyophthirius, also known as Ich or white spot, attacks both cold water and tropical fishes, but it attacks tropicals much more frequently than cold water fishes. When tropical fishes were being distributed thoughout the world again after the end of the Second World War, the spread of white spot became a very serious business. Since then however, white spot, although always with us, has tended to settle down and to become rather less of a plague than it used to be, but it remains one of the most serious diseases of guppies. The causitive agent is a small one-celled animal, a protozoon, which embeds itself in the skin of the fish and there encysts and multiplies until it becomes big enough to be seen as a white pimple on the surface of the fish. In the course of a few days this pimple enlarges and bursts and the parasite drops to the bottom of the tank where it again forms a cyst which produces up to 2,000 young, these eventually hatch out and become free-swimming in the water and attach to fishes to start the cycle once more. The process takes only eight or ten days in the tropical aquarium, but at lower temperatures it may last very much longer.

The parasite penetrates the mucus coat and the outer layers of the epidermis of the fish and remains active, moving about in the blister that it causes. The epidermis of the fish is irritated and reacts by forming a bladder which is a pathological symptom of the disease. The parasite feeds on red blood corpuscles and disintegrating cells; the irritation occasioned by the parasite causes the fish to scrub itself on plants and other objects in the tank and this may occur before white spots become visible. They may have also settled in the gills and caused the fish distress even to the extent of gasping in respiration before many, or any, white spots are visible on the surface of the fish. It will be recognized that the water constantly passing over the gill plates of the fish afford the parasite an excellent opportunity for settling down there in the first instance. As the untreated infestation increases, the guppy will become heavily covered with white spots, first on the fins, then on the whole of the body. Some tropical fishes may be almost completely covered by white spot disease, yet not show very great evidence of distress, but the guppy is a fish which is particularly susceptible to the toxicity of white spot disease and it may die before a heavy infestation stage is reached.

White spot disease is found endemic in the waters of the United States and the continent of Europe; it was not found in England in the wild until quite recently, but unfortunately it now infects the wild fish in Britain. The disease is extremely contagious and must be guarded against once it appears; nothing should leave the aquarium which is contaminated by white spot without careful sterilization. It is very likely that the average tank is already infested by the white spot parasite although it may remain in a relatively dormant condition unless the fishes are chilled, over-crowded, or otherwise abused. Then it may burst forth in a sudden phase of activation and rapid measures have to be taken to prevent its spread. There has been a good deal of argument about

Best-of-show award winners at 1969 show in Long Beach, California: breeders classes, half-black female, and (facing page) bi-color male. Midge Hill photos. Following color photos (through page 93) are award winners at the 1968 International Guppy Show in Vienna, photographed by Dr. Karl Knaack. All are first place winners except as noted.

the extent to which the white spot parasite can occur in tap water; in areas where the water is heavily chlorinated or otherwise disinfected, this is not a severe danger, but in areas where the water is only filtered or treated by very mild measures white spot can be transferred from tap water to the aquarium. Even though a new fish appears perfectly healthy and free of any suspicion of white spot,

HALF-BLACK
FEMALE

it should be recalled that it may be carrying the parasites inside its gills and that despite not being visible they will be capable of infecting any tank of fishes into which introduced. This is one of the reasons why quarantine of new specimens is essential.

There are quite a number of remedies advocated as suitable for the cure of white spot; these include treatment by raising the temperature of the aquarium water up to as much as 90°F, treatment with various drugs such as mercurochrome, methylene blue, quinine, or even common salt, and treatment by the antibiotics. None of these

BI-COLOR
DELTA

treatments appears to do very much towards killing the parasites as long as they are embedded in the skin of the fish. However, they don't stay there very long and in the course of a few days the parasites will drop off and fall to the bottom of the tank. It is when they hatch out after having formed cysts at the bottom of the tank and become free-swimming organisms that the attack of the chemical is successful. Heat treatment doesn't seem to be much more than an auxillary hurry-up mechanism. The chemical substances mentioned (such as Mercurochrome and methylene blue) attack the parasites and kill them. Methylene blue is quite effective but it colors everything deeply blue; if plants are present, it stains them rather badly and it even stains the fishes themselves. For this reason it isn't the best drug to advise, but it is effective.

The drug of choice would appear to be quinine, best given as the hydrochloride, which is fairly soluble in water. If the hydrochloride is not obtainable, the less soluble quinine sulphate may be used. The dose recommended is two grains per gallon (which is 30 mg per litre) or 1 part per 30,000. It is dissolved in a liberal quantity of water prior to being placed in the tank and is added to the tank in three equal doses at about twelve hour intervals. If necessary the treatment may be repeated a week or so later without having to change the water. Unfortunately, some plants are susceptible to quinine and may not survive, particularly a repeat dose. *Vallisneria* is such a plant and it is likely to be lost during heavy quinine treatment. However, the majority of aquarium plants will survive the drug. The water may go slightly cloudy but this will be about the worst effect the quinine will have. It is advisable to change the water at the end of the period of treatment (about two weeks after giving the first dose) in order to get rid of residual quinine which may have a bad effect on fishes if left for a prolonged period. It is particularly suspected of causing partial sterility.

Do not expect the white spot to disappear by the next day; the parasites embedded in the skin of the fish are not going to be much affected and new white spots may even appear for the next two or three days as new invisible infestations will grow to become visible spots. At the end of about three days the fishes should begin to clear up and all signs of infestation should have disappeared by eight or ten days; if it hasn't, a repeat dose of quinine should be given. Fortunately, the treatment is usually effective at the first attempt and has no ill effect on the fishes. It is unfortunate however, that moving apparently cured fishes from the tank to a different environment often brings on a new attack, showing that the pest has not really been completely eradicated. An important point is not to give smaller doses of quinine than recommended in the hope that they will prove effective; they will not.

Rust or Velvet Disease

The post-war epidemics of white spot disease abated more or less and were replaced by epidemics of rust disease, so called because it resembles a dusting of fine yellowish powder over the surface of the fish, giving it indeed a rusty appearance. The disease is particularly dangerous to fry or very young fishes, it is not usually fatal to their parents. It is very easy therefore for the breeders to infect their young and for batch after batch of these to be killed by the disease. Velvet disease is rather difficult to see until the infestation becomes heavy and it may therefore go undetected in the earlier phases and be a serious menace by the time it is seen. Unlike white spot, the spots are not completely motionless and may be seen to wave gently on the surface of the fish. The main differences from white spot are this movement, the smaller size of the spots, and their yellowish appearance. Some strains of a different organism however are white, making it even more difficult to distinguish it from white spot itself.

The condition is caused by one of two species of the organism *Oodinium*. In the United States *Oodinium limneticum* is the main causative organism, but elsewhere the disease appears normally to be caused by *Oodinium pillularis*. A very similar disease in marine fishes is caused by a third organism, *Oodinium ocellatum*. The parasite has a cycle similar to that of white spot and is caused by a

HALF-BLACK
TRIANGLE

dinoflagellate protozoon. The dinoflagellates have whip-like flagellae with which they swim, and by a flagellum is the mode of attachment to the fish. After having stuck onto the fish with this flagellum, the organism sinks into the surface tissues and pushes out pseudopodia like an amoeba, forms a cyst, and eventually this bursts to free about 200 new young parasites. As with white spot it is most easily killed in the free-swimming stage, but quinine is not of use with *Oodinium*. Other chemicals such as methylene blue have been advocated but are not entirely certain in their effectiveness and also have the drawback of staining the tank and rendering the water almost impossible to see into to observe progress.

The preferable treatment is with copper. Any soluble salt of copper such as the sulphate or citrate may be

RED
TRIANGLE

GREEN
TRIANGLE

used and is rapidly fatal to velvet disease parasites. In fresh water, copper sulphate is quite satisfactory although it tends to precipitate out in marine water. Treatment has to be given very carefully because copper is toxic to fishes as well as to the parasite. Before the exact dosage had been worked out, it used to be the custom to place copper coins or to hang copper gauze in the aquarium and to watch carefully to note when the parasite had been killed and to remove the coins or gauze before the fishes were also affected. This is a dangerous technique; it had to be used before we knew the proper dosage to employ, but it certainly should not be used any longer. The effective dose of copper is 0.4 parts per million of the copper ion; this is equivalent to 2 parts per million or 7 mg per gallon of blue crystalline copper sulphate.

VARICOLORED
TRIANGLE

If a solution of copper sulphate is used, a 1% solution in distilled water will keep almost indefinitely and should be added in a total dose of not more than 1 ml per gallon. However, it is best to divide this dose for administration over a two or three day period, say a third of the dose on each of three days and withholding the third dose if the cure appears to be progressing satisfactorily. Copper acts on the fishes, causing them to secrete a copious mucus which helps to eliminate the parasite from the surface of the body and to prevent more from attaching themselves. Thus the velvet may appear to be cured within a day or two of treatment; however, the real cure consists of the killing of the free-swimming stage by the copper and this takes somewhat longer. The fishes should therefore be watched to see that an adequate dose of copper has been given and remains in the water and that the disease does not start recurring about a week or ten days later. If an outbreak recurs, a further dose of copper is in order, but in no circumstances should the total amount of copper given exceed about 0.7 parts per million. With some fishes even this amount causes distress, loss of equilibrium, or protrusion of eyeballs, which do not persist if the copper content of the water is reduced.

Another good cure for velvet which may even be combined with the copper treatment are drugs of the acriflavine or monacrin type. They are stated by some authorities to be more toxic than chemicals commonly used, but it is doubtful that they are more toxic than copper. They are also particularly effective in the presence of salt, so that acriflavine or trypaflavine may be given in combination with about a teaspoon of salt per gallon. The dosage is the same as for copper sulphate, two parts per million; in this case however, it can be given all at once and double the quantity is safe with most fishes. The drugs should be kept in a concentrated solution, but not all forms will dissolve as readily as copper sulphate and it is not possible in some cases to have a 1% solution. A 1 in 500 or 0.2% solution is perhaps best, in which case a teaspoon per gallon (5 ml per gallon) would be a suitable dosage.

Bacterial Diseases

Various bacterial diseases cause fin degeneration, ragged spots on the fins and body, ulcers on the body, so-called mouth fungus, blood streaks on the surface of the fish or fins, and various similar conditions. These may also be treated with acriflavine, again in combination with salt as described above; they may also be treated with penicillin or a wide spectrum antibiotic. Penicillin should be given in a dose of not less than 50,000 units per gallon; it is colorless and therefore particularly advantageous to use, but it is not always effective. A useful wider spectrum antibiotic is chloromycetin which is also colorless but sometimes causes cloudiness in the water. Chloromycetin should be given in a dose of not less than 50 mg per gallon. Neither of these antibiotics harms plants and both can safely be used at several times the dosage just advocated. The only thing that mitigates against them for use in large aquariums is cost; but in the 10 gallon aquarium such as is advocated for guppy breeding the cost is not prohibitive.

Fungus

Although fungus is commoner in cold water fishes it can still attack the guppy. It will follow subsequent to injury or damage of tissues by disease and will even occur as a result of poor health or bad tank conditions such as overcrowding. Fungus spores are always present in the aquarium and it is not possible to eliminate them; however, fungus attacks only injured or unhealthy fishes. There are various species of fungus which are airborne and fall into the tank, not by any means always *Saprolegnia*, which is usually named as the causative organism.

**GOLD
DOUBLE-SWORD**

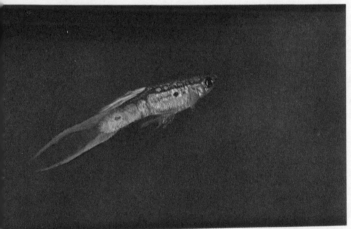

GRAY
DOUBLE-SWORD

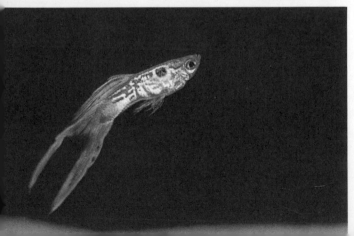

**VIENNA
EMERALD
DOUBLE-SWORD**

EMERALD
LOWER
SWORDTAIL

Fishes affected by fungus display whitish, fuzzy areas resembling dabs of cotton wool, or they may show only a fairly flat surface coating, particularly in the earlier phases of an attack. If it is not treated, the fungus will spread, destroying tissues of the affected fish. However, it will not usually spread to other fishes unless they are also damaged or unhealthy. Treatment for fungus is therefore to net out the affected fish and treat for a brief period in a bath of brilliant green or malachite green, which should be of medically pure quality and free of zinc. Use a solution of 1 in 15,000 (60 mg per litre, or 4 grains per gallon) and place the fish into it for half a minute, no longer. After treatment the fish may be replaced in the original tank; the fungus will be deeply colored by the dye and will usually drop off in the course of the next day or so. If treatment is not completely successful, it may be repeated without harm.

GRAY
LOWER
SWORDTAIL

The above afflictions are those which can mainly be expected in the guppy tank. Guppies should not suffer attacks of gill flukes or gill worms, nor be infested by other parasites. These are only introduced by careless handling of food or by fishes caught in the wild. If the guppies appear sick and it has not been possible to establish exactly why they are sick, it is safe to give them treatment with acriflavine or monacrin together with salt, or to treat with a medium dose of penicillin. Such treatment often effects a cure even though we do not know the organism that has been responsible for the disease. The important thing is to learn to distinguish white spot from velvet disease because treatment which is effective against one is not effective against the other. The avoidance of overcrowding, with cleanliness and good feeding will usually assure healthy fish. If sickness does occur, act promptly; don't wait to see what happens or you will witness the death of some of your fishes.

Various aquarium remedies are available at your petshop. Often the application of one of these chemicals might cause the death of your guppies because the drugs react with other chemicals in the water and the guppies cannot take the chemical shock. In all cases it is preferable to treat sick fish in isolated aquariums rather than treating the entire tank. Buy your drugs from your aquarium store where you can get good advice and fresh drugs.

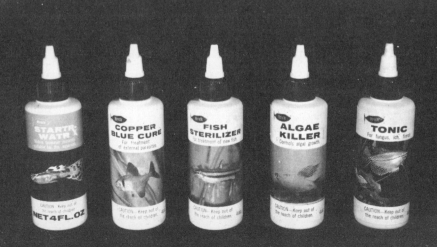

New York Zoological Society photo of guppy with hereditary lardosis; destroy such a fish or bent spines will
appear in future generations.

Magnification showing detail of anal fin construction of the male gonopodium,
the parts of which are held to form a duct through which packets of sperm
are transferred to the female. Le Cuziat photo.

Enlargement of a Le Cuziat photo of a female guppy's gravid spot, the area
by the anal fin where the dark wall of the peritoneum shows through the skin.
Imminent expulsion of a youngster is evidenced as an eye is plainly visible
through the body wall of the mother.

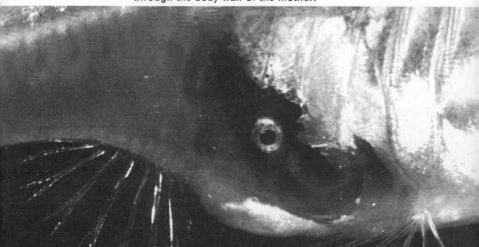

THREE-QUARTERS
BLACK FANTAIL

GREEN
FANTAIL

RED FANTAIL

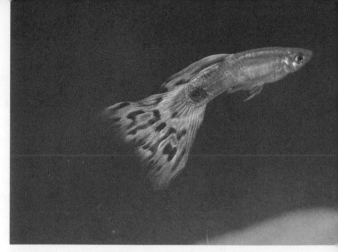

VARICOLORED
FANTAIL

HALF-BLACK
FANTAIL

FEMALE

7. GUPPY GENETICS

Body and fin colors, body size and shape, fin size and shape, and even behavior in the guppy depend upon heredity. The genes (carried on the chromosomes) are the agents influencing these characteristics.

Some characteristics in animals (and plants) depend upon the action of a single gene, or hereditary factor. In the guppy, the gene for golden body coloration is such a factor. Such factors may be dominant or recessive to each other; the grey wild type is in this instance dominant to the golden type. This means that any individual must have a double dose of the gene for gold coloration in order to appear golden. If it does not inherit the golden gene both from its father and its mother, it will be grey in appearance even though the gene from one parent is a golden determinant. Thus a stock of pure golden guppies has only the gene for gold and none of the normal wild type genes which would give the members of the stock a grey appearance.

In the diagram, both the egg and the sperm cells carry the gene for golden, represented by the small letter g. The offspring can therefore only be golden in color as the gene for golden has been inherited from both sides.

$$gg \qquad \times \qquad gg$$

Golden female   Golden male
Ova: g Sperm: g
F_1 offspring: all gg (independent of sex)
Appearance: golden. (Generations produced in a breeding program are designated F for filial, and are numbered in sequence.)

If we take a wild type guppy and represent his grey coloration by the capital G, then the normal wild type guppy will have inherited this from both parents and so his genetic constitution as regards body color will be represented by *GG*. All of the offspring from males and females with this wild type characteristic cannot be other than wild type in color. However, if we mate a wild type guppy with a golden guppy the following situation occurs:

$$GG \qquad \times \qquad gg$$

Grey female   Golden male

Ova: *G*   Sperm: *g*

F_1 offspring: All *Gg* (independent of sex)

Appearance: grey

One parent whether male or female (it doesn't matter which) contributes a gene *G* to the offspring, while the other donates a gene *g* to the offspring. All of the offspring will therefore be of the genetic constitution *Gg* and will be grey in colour because the gene for grey is dominant over the gene for golden. An amateur breeder might well be disappointed at this and imagine that the offspring were quite useless because the golden color had entirely disappeared. However, if he were to go further and mate the offspring together the following situation would be seen from crossing such F_1 individuals.

$$Gg \qquad \times \qquad Gg$$

Grey female   Grey male (but heterozygous for *g*).

Ova: *G* and *g*   Sperm *G* and *g* (both in equal proportions)

F_2 offspring: $\frac{1}{4}$ *GG*, $\frac{1}{2}$ *Gg*, $\frac{1}{4}$ *gg*

Appearance: $\frac{3}{4}$ grey, $\frac{1}{4}$ golden

We see that one quarter of the offspring of the first generation of wild type mated to golden guppies will show gold once more; this is because of a phenomenon called segregation in which the genes sort themselves out so that one quarter of the offspring will be *gg*, and therefore golden in appearance. It will also be noted that

BRONZE-GREEN
FANTAIL

GOLD FANTAIL

BLUE FANTAIL

GOLD
LOWER
SWORDTAIL

BLUE
TRIANGLE

VEILTAIL

Guppies and water sprite, photo by Dr. Herbert R. Axelrod. The large number that can be kept in limited space makes the colorful and active guppy a favorite with hobbyists.

a third of the grey guppies (one-fourth of the total number of fry) will be homozygous, or pure-bred for the G gene. The remaining two-thirds (half of all the fry) are heterozygous, which means that they each have Gg in their makeup.

Sex-limited and Sex-linked Inheritance

Some genes can only show expression in one sex. In the case of the guppy, many color genes manifest themselves only in the male; so also do many genes affecting finnage characteristics. Thus the male guppy can be colorful with long flowing fins of different shapes, whereas the females characteristically have rounded fins and little or no coloration but grey is visible. There are some strains in which the females are colorful, but these are exceptional and have been specially and painstakingly bred. The reason that the male guppy can show finnage changes and color changes is that his male sex hormone (testosterone) facilitates the actual showing of the color and of the finnage types that his genes carry. The female may carry the same genes but she does not show the effect of them, at least not the external effect that they have on color and finnage. This type of inheritance is known as sex-limited because its visible expression is normally limited to one sex.

The second type of inheritance is sex-linked. This means that the particular gene or genes in question are carried on the sex chromosomes and therefore they will show in one sex and not in the other. In the guppy as in ourselves, a male has an X chromosome and a Y chromosome, the female has two X chromosomes. The male produces two sorts of sperm, one bearing a Y chromosome and the other bearing an X chromosome. The female produces eggs of one type only, all contain X chromosomes; it can therefore be seen that the sex of the offspring depends upon the particular sperm which fertilizes an egg. If a sperm bearing an X chromosome fertilizes the egg, the offspring will be XX, a female. If a sperm bearing a Y chromosome fertilizes the egg the offspring will be XY, a male. Furthermore, genes that are carried on the Y chromosome can only show up in the male since the female doesn't have a Y chromosome. This is an example of sex-linked inheritance which is also seen in some of the color characteristics of the guppy.

Inheritance of More Than One Factor

A recessive gene (as is the one for golden) is the gene for veiltail. This is a sex-limited gene (which golden is not) and finds expression only in the male guppy, being therefore both recessive and sex-limited. If we have a pure veiltail stock, the fish must be homozygous for veiltail which we will represent by v while using V to represent the wild round-tail stock. Such veiltail guppies must all be vv in constitution and mating between them can only give rise to v stock. If we cross a wild type guppy with the

ROUNDTAIL

FLAMINGO
SPADETAIL

PINTAIL

RED
SPADETAIL

POINTED-TAIL

FORM (balanced
conformation)

veiltail guppy, all of the first generation offspring (denoted by F_1) will be wild type in appearance, grey and round-tailed. If we mate these F_1 guppies, the next generation (F_2) will be one quarter vv offspring, but only in the male will this be visible. All of the females will look like the wild type, but one quarter of the males (one-eighth of all the offspring) will show veiltail once more. This is shown schematically in the diagram:

VV $\times$ vv

Round-tail female   Veiltail male

Ova: V Sperm: v

F_1 offspring: All Vv (independent of sex)

Appearance: round tail

Vv $\times$ Vv

Round-tail female   Round-tail male

Ova: V and v Sperm: V and v (in equal proportions)

F_2 offspring: VV: $2Vv$: vv (but vv apparent only in males)

Appearance: All females round-tail; $\frac{1}{4}$ of males veiltail

But suppose we have a stock of golden guppies and we have another stock of veiltail guppies and we wish to produce golden veiltails. How do we do it? Obviously we have to start by mating the golden guppies to the veiltail guppies. The golden are homozygous for gold but have the wild-type gene in the tail-shape position; whereas the veiltail guppies are homozygous for veiltail but have the corresponding wild-type gene in the color position. This is represented in the diagram:

$ggVV$ $\times$ $GGvv$

Golden female   Veiltail male

Ova: all gV Sperm: all Gv

F_1 offspring: All $GgVv$ (independent of sex)

Appearance: Wild-type-grey, round-tailed

Things can now be seen to be getting a bit more complicated; all of the offspring of this cross will be wild type in appearance; none of them will be golden; none of them will be veiltail, and once again the amateur breeder might be very disappointed and downcast by the result of this cross because he might not realise that the desired combination of genes can be recovered from such an unpromising first cross. However, let's see what happens when we cross the F_1 fish to produce an F_2 generation. The result is shown below:

$$GgVv \qquad \times \qquad GgVv$$

Wild-type female   Wild-type male

Ova: GV, Gv, gV, gv Sperm: GV, Gv, gV, gv

F_2 Offspring: $GGVV$; $2GGVv$; $GGvv$; $2GgVV$ $4GgVv$; $2Ggvv$; $ggVV$; $2ggVv$; $ggvv$ in ratio

Appearance males: color—$\frac{3}{4}$ (1 or $2G$) grey, $\frac{1}{4}$ (gg) golden; tail shape—$\frac{3}{4}$ (1 or $2V$) round-tail, $\frac{1}{4}$ (vv) veiltail [of which $\frac{1}{16}$ ($ggvv$) will be golden and veiltailed)

females: $\frac{3}{4}$ wild-type, $\frac{1}{4}$ golden

As before, one quarter of the offspring will be golden, and one-quarter of the offspring will be genetically veiltails although the sex-limited gene manifests itself only in the males. As a result one-eighth of the offspring (males) will be veiltail as to appearance. If we assume that these two genes are segregating at random (that is they are not both near together on the same chromosome, which would be a complication), we can anticipate that one-quarter of one-eighth (one-thirty-second) of the offspring will be males which are both veiltail and are golden. These are obviously the fish that we want, but what do we do about the females?

We can segregate the golden females, but we cannot select the ones bearing veiltail genes unless we use a special technique, using hormones to reveal the genetic constitution of the female. In the case of the veiltail, this

GOLD FANTAIL

VARICOLORED
TRIANGLE

RED FANTAIL

FLAMINGO
SPADETAIL

Albino guppies are not very popular since albinism, by definition, is the lack of black chromatophores (pigment cells). This albino guppy was bred in Czechoslovakia where it was photographed by Dr. Stanislav Frank.

The fish below and those on the facing page were judged second in their class at the 1969 show in Vienna.

would not be very practical, as it happens, because it would require too long an exposure to the hormone. We therefore have to mate the golden veiltail males to all of the golden females, one quarter of which will be golden veiltail females. Therefore in a quarter of such crosses we will be getting pure golden veiltail stock. By proper management we can detect which females are carrying the genes we desire and can recover from the created mixture the particular males and females desired for further matings. The point at this stage is that by proper use of a knowledge of inheritance it is possible to combine such characters as desired.

Physiology of some colors

In the discussion of golden guppies and the wild type grey guppies, no explanation was given regarding the differences between the two types. If we look at the skin of the wild type grey guppy, particularly in the female, it will be noted that the grey is overlaid by other colors; we see that there are many small cells containing a pigment (melanin) which is black or very dark brown in color. The cells themselves are called melanophores. In many species of lower vertebrates (such as the frog) and in some species of marine fishes (such as the skate), these melanophores are highly contractile cells. Pigment is dispersed throughout the body of the expanded cell and coloring is distinct; but little or no color is perceptible when such a cell is contracted.

In the guppy this dispersion of pigment may occur only to a limited degree. Against a dark background the melanophores disperse their pigment and expand; against a light background the pigment is contracted and the guppy looks lighter. This color-change reflex involves vision and a blind guppy cannot react in this manner.

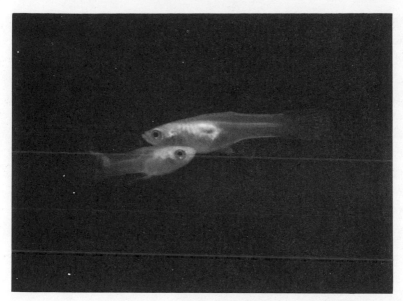

A pair of gold guppies photographed by Mervin F. Roberts.

The golden guppy has only about half the number of melanophores that are present in the wild guppy. This is an effect of the mutation to golden; another consequence is that a guppy possessing the mutation exposes more of the cells underlying the melanophores (which are xanthophores and contain yellow pigment) and thus the yellow of the golden guppy is observed. (Although melanophores of the golden guppy are somewhat larger than those of a normal guppy, they are so much fewer in number that the effect does not balance out.)

There is a guppy (called blond), which is even lighter than the golden guppy and a different situation obtains here. The skin of the blond guppy has about the same number of melanophores as that of the wild type, but the cells are small and not capable of expansion to the normal extent, and so are unable to blanket the cells containing the golden pigment even to the extent that this can occur in the golden guppy. Therefore the blond mutant appears more yellow and more translucent than the golden guppy.

95

Sometimes female guppies are dosed with hormones to detect color patterns
carried by the genes, or for show purposes, and continued drug administration
may produce advanced development of male characteristics. Whether or not
such a gonopodial conformation as shown in this Zukal photograph is capable
of function as an intromittent organ is a disputed subject.

The two effects are produced by different mutants acting in a different way to reduce the possibility of the melanin pigment being spread out as a blanket over the skin and giving it the darker greyish appearance of the wild guppy.

In the albino guppy we have a rather different type of mutant. The albino guppy completely lacks melanin. The lack of pigmentation makes visible the reddish glow of the blood supplying the eyes and they are seen as pink. It doesn't matter whether the guppy also has the gene for grey, or gold, or any other color because the effect of pairing the albino determining gene is to prevent the development of any pigment and it neutralizes the effect of any other color regulating genes that may be present. Albinism is caused by recessive genes and they must be paired to be effective; moreover, other genes affecting coloration (even though themselves recessive) are dominant over those for albinism, thus accounting for the rare appearance of albinos in natural populations.

Three ways in which a guppy may be paler than normal have been discussed, each involving genes producing a different effect on the melanin carried in the skin of the normal wild type fish. One might expect that these three genes, color regulators for golden, blond, and albino, would form a so-called allelomorphic series and perhaps all exist on the same locus (or place) on a chromosome. Although this situation is definitely seen in some series, as in genes affecting eye colors of the *Drosophila* fruit fly, it happens that in the guppy these genes are on different loci, not necessarily even on the same chromosome, and exert their effects quite independently.

The other pigments present, particularly in the male guppy, are of course responsible for the intensely vivid coloration that males of certain strains possess. In addition to having melanophores and xanthophores, these guppies have other cells called chromatophores which contain red pigment, blue pigment, and other so-far incompletely described pigments. These are not usually contractile cells in the way that the melanophores may be contractile, but sometimes they are capable of expansion and contraction to a considerable degree. This phenomenon is seen when drugs such as reserpine are added in very minute quantities to the food or water. Reserpine has a very spectacular effect when food containing it is fed to the guppy male. At one time it was said that unless show guppies were fed reserpine-containing food there really was not much hope for them to win awards because they would appear quite dull and dingy in comparison with drugged competitors. It is not very clear at this time as to what extent this practice has been continued; certainly many of our modern guppy strains are so brilliant that it is difficult to imagine that drugs could enhance their coloration.

From what has been said, it will also be realized that since the genes for albino, blond, and golden are on different parts of the hereditary apparatus, mating any two stocks of these together will give a first generation which are wild type in appearance, and to recover any of the genes from such a cross, it will be necessary to go on, at least to the next generation when the phenomenon of segregation may be expected to result in a proportion of the F_2 showing the mutant characteristics once more so that combinations of them may be arranged.

Further genetics

It will be seen that an understanding of single gene inheritance in the guppy is an important part of the necessary knowledge for guppy breeding. We know a fair amount about the inheritance of the characteristics important to the present day breeder of fancy guppies, but there are some big gaps in our knowledge which need to be closed. Here for instance, is a recent listing of the dominant and recessive characteristics of some genes controlling color and tail-fin characteristics, and some of the body size characteristics of the guppy:

Dominant	Recessive
Wild type grey	Blond
Wild type grey	Golden
Golden	Blond
Wild type grey	Albino
Round tail	Pointed tail
Round tail	Bannertail
Round tail	Veiltail
Round tail	Swordtail
Absence of sword	Swordtail
Wild type tail	Black spots on tail in female
Wild type tail	Checkerboard pattern in female
Normal growth	Giantism
Dwarfism	Giantism
Zebrinus	Wild type

It will be noted that nearly all the genes influencing desirable body color, tail shape other than normal, and spots on the tail, and large sized body are recessive to the normal or wild type. Only zebrinus is dominant to the wild type in the listing. This is quite a normal situation; it indicates however that the combination of desirable characteristics when these are recessive requires a rather tedious amount of breeding and recovering indicated in the preceding discussion.

A considerable amount of work can be done (and of course much has been done in the past) in the establishment of strains by the combination of various desirable characteristics. However, if one had originally only individual mutants in different strains, a very complicated and protracted program would be required to combine all of these in logical mating patterns to develop the type of guppy most desired. Even when a single new gene (as the cobra gene recently described in *TFH* magazine) appears, it may require 50 or 60 tanks of breeders to get this gene in homozygous form and then to combine it and recombine it with existing stocks possessing a combination of other desirable genes. While it is therefore possible to follow a program of genetic inbreeding and segregation of the type needed to isolate and combine the desirable genes, it must be recognised that this is a very time consuming, space consuming, and tedious business. Nevertheless, this is how guppy strains have in the course of years been brought to their present development. As new genic effects were found, some of them have been seized upon by enthusiasts or professional breeders and have been combined into existing guppy stocks so as to improve them and add variety to that which was already in existence.

It is however unfortunate that a process of close inbreeding is a necessary part of such development. Offspring of the F_1 and F_2 generations of such brother-sister matings may be quite disappointing. The fixation of the desired genes may be accompanied by deterioration in the general stock so that the desirable genes may be accumulated in otherwise very scruffy-looking fish. In order to avoid this, any process of inbreeding and cross-breeding is best accompanied by a degree of out-crossing. Alternately a number of lines of inbred fish possessing the desired characteristics must be maintained at the same time so there will be at least one or two populations of fish which do not show deterioration and from which selection for further breeding can be made. It is possible to produce highly inbred strains which are healthy, vigorous fishes, but it isn't normal for this to occur and the result of varying degrees of inbreeding is usually the opposite. We shall discuss further on how this may be avoided, but in the earlier stages of fixing certain genes into existing stocks it cannot be completely avoided.

The best animals are often produced by crossing two inbred lines with the result that in a certain proportion of cases the F_1 generation shows a phenomenon known as hybrid vigour and may be truly magnificent and uniform creatures. These if then bred together may produce such a great variety of desirable and undesirable, mediocre and even dreadful fishes that it would not be a method advocated for the start of a new line of fishes. However, if the breeder has sufficient ambition and the capacity to maintain and test a number of inbred lines so that the best of the F_1 crosses between them can be decided and then regularly produced, he may in fact be able to produce superb fishes. No instance is known in which this has been done with the guppy itself but it is a common practice in the breeding of poultry and development of certain plants and will no doubt spread eventually into the realm of the fish breeder. The big advantage to the producer is that he is the only one who can produce the magnificent animals that he will offer for sale; when the purchaser wishes to replenish his stock, he must go back to the original source, since the F_1 fishes that he possesses will show the phenomenon of segregation discussed above when he tries to breed them to one another. It would be a major program for him to attempt to recover by further selective breeding the desirable characteristics shown in the F_1 generation from which he will have to start.

A pair of veiltails photographed by Dave Freidman.

8. SELECTION WITH MINIMAL IN-BREEDING

Once the ordinary breeder is able to obtain a good stock of guppies and is concerned mainly with improving this strain, or at least maintaining it in its present state of excellence, the problem is no longer one of inbreeding or genetic recombination. It is instead a problem of keeping good guppies as good as they are and if possible making them better. The technique to be used is a group-mating program and does not necessarily require a very large number of fish. The optimum conditions for keeping a few guppies are also the best conditions for a program of breeding which avoids any significant degree of inbreeding.

Significant strides in the production of first class guppies have only been made since too rigid an adherence to sets of standards has been abandoned. If the aim is producing a guppy to an ideal standard, which shall have such-and-such a finnage, such-and-such body-shape, and so-on and so-forth, it is very hard to select for all of these points and to maintain good colour, good body size, and good finnage. The more factors one tries to select for simultaneously in any rigid kind of manner, the more almost impossibly difficult it becomes to make an effective selection of breeders. This is why it is advisable merely to start a program of general improvement. If anything good turns up in the form of a new fin type or distinctive coloration, it should be seized upon to be perpetuated through further breeding. But it is better to hold what is good than to try to improve on it and sacrifice desirable characteristics in striving to fix a particular one.

Instead of imposing some arbitrary standard on our breeding, we should take advantage of what nature gives us and seize on anything good that turns up and in so doing can expect to make very much greater strides. This is what American and German aquarists in particular have at last realized and are practicing. They no longer strive after some theoretical ideal shape, size, or coloration of fishes. It has been proved more productive to take every advantage of anything good that turns up in coloring, exciting new finnage, or new patterning, any of which may just appear out of the blue and should be selected, improved upon as far as possible, and may perhaps lead to development of a strain of fish which is unexpectedly beautiful yet does not conform to any particular preconceived ideas. Such a product can be obtained because there are always dozens of so-called modifier genes which will intensify or detract from the effects of one or more of the genes effecting major character development. A delta tail can be broadened or narrowed within reason by the effects of these modifier genes. If one attempts however to accumulate modifiers to narrow the tail and lengthen it out to a ribbon tail, intense activity in this direction will probably result in loss of some desirable characteristics in the stock. However, in various fishes these modifier genes will always be acting and can be accumulated in such manner that they may produce a desirable fish without any adverse effect upon desirable characteristics which we may wish to retain. It should be remarked that the accumulation of such modifying genes is best achieved by the group mating of the type described in the following discussion. Single pairs of fishes will not be able to offer the possibilities of genetic recombination or accumulation of small-effect genes which the group mating system offers.

The group mating system is often called "line breeding," which is a rather diluted type of inbreeding, purposely diluted so that the worst effects of inbreeding are avoided. In essence, selection is made of a few pairs of fish from a particular batch (usually only from a single batch but not necessarily so) and the random mating of these fishes is permitted in a standard aquarium, the total number of fish usually being confined to fewer than about a dozen. There may be equal numbers of males and females but it is general practice to use twice as many females as males. These breeders are then left to mate freely. From the hundreds of offspring that they will produce, a similar group (or more often several groups) of up to about a dozen fish will be carefully selected for further mating. One batch may be selected for the tail shape, another for a different characteristic. If there has suddenly appeared a number of male guppies with black bodies or some other desirable characteristic they will be segregated and mated with some of their sisters in the hope of maintaining and fixing the characteristic. The main point however is that a small batch consisting of young particularly selected from moderately close relatives is bred to avoid direct inbreeding yet at the same time to start the accumulation of desirable genes and their modifiers in breeding stocks aimed at developing a strain of fish with different but desirable characteristics. The rest, more than 95% probably, of their brothers and sisters will be sold or discarded.

Such line breeding is the method used by Hahnel, Sternke, and many other outstanding breeders. When practiced as recommended, the system entails a process of meticulous selection with necessarily quite ruthless culling of all undesirable fish. It also encompasses a continual scrutiny of progeny to assure that the offspring of a group of breeders are as desirable or more attractive than the parental stock. If they are not, it is obviously pointless to continue the course of breeding. Not all attractive parents produce attractive offspring and not all desirable offspring are the products of attractive parents. Generally we shall select only distinctive parents for breeding under the line breeding scheme, but we must at least give ourselves the opportunity of seeing to what extent their offspring are as desirable or more so than they are. Those groups of parents that produce offspring that are not desirable must themselves be discarded and new groups substituted for them. By this method, the breeder gets the best out of his tanks and does not waste too much time in the propagation of lines of fish that display nothing more than ordinary characteristics. This system of selective propagation is important. Parents that have proved to produce desirable young are mated and the breeder goes on breeding from batches of their young and discards all lines of fish which are not desirably productive. Remember that the female guppy does not usually show much of the coloration that will be seen in the male, and that it is the characters of the male for which we are primarily breeding. Therefore, progeny testing of females is highly important since in normal circumstances what they have to offer in genetic characteristics is not visible.

It will be appreciated that even line breeding requires a considerable number of tanks. The fewer the tanks the aquarist possesses, the more limited his program must necessarily be. A breeder with only half a dozen 10 to 20 gallon tanks must virtually confine himself to trying to keep and perfect not more than one stock of guppies. At least three tanks will be needed for each run of a line breeding program, and this is a minimal figure. A start must be made with a guaranteed stock of good guppies from a reputable source, needless to say, and we must be sure that the females belong to the same strain as the males, an unholy confusion may be produced in the very first generation. Unfortunately, some guppy suppliers mix females of one stock with males from another one with exactly that purpose in mind. One must avoid any chance of this occurring; try therefore to obtain at least half a dozen young guppies from a reputable source. Do not hesitate to pay a premium price to ensure that you get what you really want. Mate them as a small group and see what their progeny are like. If the first

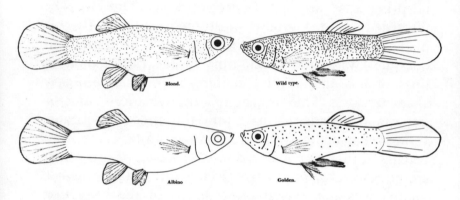

Diagram showing distribution of melanophores (pigmentation cells) of guppy strains.

young are not quite as good as their parents, this is almost to be expected. Naturally, you will have asked for and one supposes obtained some of the very best of the stock from which a start is to be made, and the average for that stock will probably be decidedly below that which you obtained at this beginning of a line breeding program. Therefore, you must expect a small drop in average quality of the young and be very pleased if you don't get it. Any significant drop however, should alert you to the possibility that this is a poor stock from which to make a start.

Assuming that no marked drop in quality has occurred, the next step is to select two groups from the first generation of young guppies for further mating. These two mating groups are put into separate tanks and each will consist of up to about a dozen young parents. They and their progeny are to be tested and treated in exactly the same manner. One can see how rapidly it is possible to expand the number of tanks utilized in a single project of this type and if the tank number is to be strictly limited, earlier parental generations will have to be discarded as soon as it is feasible to do so. The progress that is made by this type of breeding will naturally depend on the genetic constitution as well as the environment provided for the fish in question. The breeder gambles on the genes of the original half dozen or so guppies from which the particular program is started. If the genetic make-up is revealed to be unsatisfactory, a new start will have to be made with other stock.

With any normal stock of prize-winning guppies, the progeny will be attractive and further progress in development can be expected along whatever selection line has been determined upon by the breeder. Keeping accurate records of what is going on is essential. Without records, it is very easy to forget exactly which tank of guppies is which and to get the whole breeding program in a state of confusion. Geneticists keep individual records of the animals they are breeding and know precisely the performance of each male and female. In the line breeding system, we cannot do this, but we can keep careful records of the performance of groups of guppies, as though they were individuals.

If any degree of inbreeding is to be practiced, it is necessary to establish a detailed card index system. On these cards it is necessary to record the segregation of genes and the genetic combinations observed in each individual batch of guppies from each individual pair

Ruda Zukal photo of an intricately patterned double-sword male and his drab mate.

of parents. This provides information about the nature of the genes with which we were experimenting and about the viability of the offspring carrying particular genes. Even if a ratio of say 3 to 1 wild type to another type is expected in a particular mating, this may not be maintained because the other type might be less vigorous than the wild type and therefore not survive so well. This would be noted in the form of a departure from a 3:1 ratio giving some lower ratio instead. An extreme example of this is demonstrated by the gene for albinism; albinos are rarely kept as a pure breeding stock because of the poor viability of the albino guppy. Instead, the albinos are usually produced from heterozygotes of wild type appearance and the albino young are separated from their more vigorous brothers and sisters at a very early age and are raised separately.

9. REVERSION TO
OR TOWARDS TYPE

There are two ways in which fancy guppies may revert to type. One is very rapid, the other a slower process. If we cross unrelated guppy strains, we run the risk in the first generation of immediately losing the manifestation of recessive genes that are not present in both stocks. Thus if we crossed a veiltail albino guppy with a swordtail blond, we would get wild type progeny because neither has the recessive gene responsible for the fancy peculiarities of the other. Strains which possess a number of recessive genes may or may not share some of these with other strains possessing similar numbers of recessive genes and the degree to which reversion occurs will therefore vary with crosses. Later generations of these crosses will show the wide range of phenotypic, that is visible genetic manifestations, expected when an F_1 generation is used for breeding.

In the absence of selective breeding measures, any strain of fancy guppies will revert to the wild type. The last thing to disappear will usually be some of the selectively developed coloration. Strains which have been bred to the point of producing almost exclusively a desired fancy type will still revert if controlled mating is not maintained. Some of the explanations of this have been mentioned. The likelihood of small-finned and runtish males effecting fertilization in random matings is a fairly obvious factor of this kind. It must also be recalled that fancy type fishes, like any fancy breed of domestic animal, are not particularly well suited for their environment and that the long flowing fins and the intense coloration typical of such breeds will tend to disappear under normal circumstances because the wild type of characteristics are those controlled by dominant genes and will reappear under natural selection. The breeder must be continually selective if he expects a good strain to be maintained or improved. Even the best Sternke or Hahnel guppies will degenerate in a relatively few generations to a very miserable population as compared with their ancestors unless they are selectively bred.

A stacked array of male guppies photographed by Dr. Herbert R. Axelrod.

10. COLOR TESTING IN THE FEMALE

We have seen that colors in guppies are normally sex-limited and that the female does not show color except in particularly developed strains. However, females carry genes which are responsible for the color of the males and these are inherited by her offspring. Since it is desirable to know what genes a female may carry and thus be capable of passing on to offspring, the technique of revealing possession of color factors by dosing her with small amounts of male hormone has become an important factor in guppy breeding. Given to females in proper concentration, the male hormone will not render them sterile or harm them in any way, yet it will exert sufficient effect to bring out the color that the females possess in their genetic constitution. The effects of the male hormone disappear after administration of the drug is stopped and the female reverts to her normal drab appearance.

We do not actually use the male hormone (testosterone) but a synthetic derivative of it called methyltestosterone. This compound is more stable in the aquarium water and therefore exerts a more prolonged effect. It is made up for administration at a strength of 3 micrograms per litre of water. Such a stock solution may be made up in the home as follows: Dissolve 100 mg of methyltestosterone in one half cup of 70% alcohol, transfer this alcoholic solution to a one quart bottle, fill the bottle with water and mix very thoroughly; this will be the stock solution for putting into the tank at 3 micrograms per liter of water.

For use in bringing out the colors carried by the female, two drops of this stock solution are added to each gallon of the aquarium water in which the females are to be treated. Two drops per gallon should be added every other day so that the gradual deterioration of this very dilute hormone solution is made up and it is kept at approximately a level strength. Do not overtreat, because sterility could result. Continue this treatment for two to four weeks, using the longer period if color does not develop after two weeks. For fully adult females it may be necessary to treat for as long as six weeks. Do not however continue beyond that time. After the colors have developed, the females may take four to six weeks to recover completely from the effects of the hormone treatment before being successfully mated.

This technique is perhaps best applied to the females of a selected group that is to be bred. It should not be used for looking at odd females which you feel may be worth breeding but which are unrelated to your currently in use stocks as it is not advisable to start crossing different guppy strains unless there is some particularly good objective behind the scheme. Within reason the younger the female the less harm will be done to her eventual breeding capacity, so that it is better to test half grown females than to do so later. Furthermore, it is both pointless and very likely to be injurious to test a female guppy more than once.

If you don't wish to breed certain females but desire to bring out the fullest possible color, an interesting result can be obtained from treating an adult female for a prolonged period. A female so treated will become male-like and develop a gonopodium. Her fins may not change very much unless very early treatment is instituted but she will develop attractive coloration.

11. STANDARDS FOR GUPPIES

American Standards

In 1957, standards for showing and judging of guppies were published in *Tropical Fish Hobbyist* magazine. These were prepared by W. L. Whitern and Herbert R. Axelrod, and they were adopted and approved by the American Federation of Guppy Societies. The standards were meant to assist and guide those who undertake to judge a competitive guppy show, and of course to guide the breeders who wish to exhibit their guppies in such a show. The introduction stated that at least twelve established varieties of guppies have been developed and pointed out that further developments in the direction of color or body shape were occurring each year. It was further pointed out that it was essential that proper classification of the many varieties of guppy be established in order that they could be accepted as entries in competitive shows, without confusion that could lead to errors when they were being judged.

The many guppy varieties were classified into the following groups: Roundtails, Speartails, Cofertails, Pintails, Lyretails, Swordtails, Scarftails and Veiltails. Color varieties of veiltails and others were designated and could be offered for competition as blue, red, green, black, or variegated. These fish could be exhibited in pairs, male and female, or two males which would then be judged on points awarded for similarity. They could also be exhibited as a collection consisting of a minimum of three pairs of any one variety, again with points to be awarded for similarity, or as a mixed collection consisting of at the least six pairs, displaying one or more varieties with no limit to the number of varieties shown. These were then to be judged as a mixed collection and not on the basis of the individual merits of members of any one variety.

Entries were also to be divided under general group coloration: grey, gold, and albino, without separate mention of blond. In the greys, the males must have a dark grey background on the body with brilliantly colored dorsal and caudal fins; other body colors on the grey might vary. The females should have a slightly lighter shade of grey than the males, with the fins streaked with color as a permissible variation. Gold males should show brilliancy of colors, all appearing on a golden-yellow body background, fins might have bright coloration; females should have a slightly lighter golden-yellow body color, clear without any overcast of other colors and with translucent finnage, although the overall body color could diffuse into the dorsal and caudal fins. In the albino, any color could exist on the fins but the eyes must be red.

Interestingly, when discussing the veiltails, the standards were set for a body length at least equal to the tail, it was remarked that too often the tail is longer than the body length, giving an impression that the body was not of sufficient strength or size to conform to a proper balance of the length of the body as against the length of the veiltail. Many prize winning modern veiltails do not conform to this standard.

A point table was outlined by which the awarding of points could be given flexibility, and yet be of assistance and guidance to the judges as shown in the standard table of points. When two males were entered for similarity judging, the better of the two was to be judged for points.

Body shape	10 points
Body size	10 points
Caudal fin shape	10 points
Caudal fin size	10 points
Dorsal fin shape	10 points
Dorsal fin size	10 points
Condition	10 points
Deportment	10 points
Color	20 points (divided with up to 5 points each possible for caudal fin, dorsal fin, body, and overall intensity)

An extra 5 points were to be given for similarity of two males and for color in the pectoral fins. A fish in good condition was defined as having a firm and well rounded body with all fins perfect and without blemishes, splits, or ragged edges. The definition of deportment laid down that the general behaviour and the display and poise and carriage of all finnage in males should be as expected, and that they should exhibit proper swimming ability.

The standards discussion included containers for entries, specifying that uniform containers should be used, that they should be of clear glass, and recommended the one gallon glass show jar as most desirable. This is of clear glass approximately 5″ square by 9″ high with a metal screw-on top which should be removed and replaced with a perforated plastic cover prior to judging. No plants, gravel, or decorations should be present. Recommendations were also made about a gallon capacity for the display of guppies in larger tanks, or for more than one day's show, with the golden rule of one guppy to one gallon of water as a guide. Pairs should be exhibited in a minimum of two gallons without any furnishings; collections should be exhibited in an aquarium of a minimum of ten gallons, with furnishings of sand and plants and aeration and filtration allowed. Mixed collection classes were to be exhibited in aquaria of not less than 29 gallons capacity with no restrictions on furnishings. Recommendations were also made about uniform standards for lighting of the entries.

Other recommendations covered an acclimatization period of at least four hours for the fish in a show and that exhibitors in the show be divided into a novice class, a semi-professional class, and a professional class. It was also remarked that since only five points for intensity of color were to be awarded, the practice of feeding stimulant foods should not cause for disqualification. It was not however recommended that stimulants be used, simply that they should not be disallowed.

German Standards

In the October 1962 issue of *Tropical Fish Hobbyist* magazine, Dr. O. M. Stoerzbach outlined the guppy standards set down by the Deutsche Guppy Gesellschaft, a group of guppy hobbyists similar to the American Guppy Association. It will be seen that these differed considerably from the American standards, and going beyond them showed actual outlines of the most desirable guppy forms and of faulty forms which were not approved for exhibit. The full points and desirable features of the various guppy types of the German standard are not outlined in this article, but the fantail guppy is taken as an illustration. Twelve diagrammatic representations of this guppy were given to illustrate desirable forms and eight illustrations were given to illustrate faulty forms. It may be added that it is sometimes quite difficult to distinguish by eye between the examples given.

Teutonic love of detail is illustrated by the text, appended to the fantail guppy illustrations. The caudal fin must form a triangle with an angle of 35° with the body; its length should approximate 8/10ths the body length; the edges should be straight although they could be slightly rounded. The dorsal fin must be very much elongated; run to a point, and end in the first third of the caudal fin. The evaluation of the caudal fin, for the length of which fifteen points were allowed, and for the form for which another fifteen points were allowed, is illustrated in the following table:

Length

8/10ths of the body length and more	Excellent	15 points
7/10ths of the body length and more	Very good	12 points
6/10ths of the body length and more	Good	9 points
5/10ths of the body length and more	No evaluation	

Angle

35° or more	Excellent	15 points
30° or more	Very good	12 points
25° or more	Good	9 points
20° or more	Fair	6 points
Less than 20°	No evaluation	

Deductible points were also enumerated:

	Deduct at least :
For the rear edge distinctly concave	1 point
For the upper & lower edge convex	2 points
For the rear edge convex	3 points
For the rear edge not square	4 points
For the caudal fin not forming an elongation of the body axis	4 points
For light irregular raggedness	1 point
For a step in the upper edge	3 points
For a defective outer edge	5 points

Further, the caudal fin could not be evaluated if it had been deformed by disease or injury, if the upper and lower edges converged flatly, or if the standard could not be definitely recognized in a particular fish. Evaluation of the dorsal fin could be to a maximum of 10 points for length and 10 points for form, with length to the first

1/3rd of the caudal fin as excellent (10 points), to the beginning of the dorsal fin as good (6 points). The form should be as outlined above, but other dorsal fin forms were to be admitted, with a deduction of at least 2 points.

The fish as a whole would have 20 points allotted for body:

Length	5 points
Form	5 points
Color	10 points

Thirty points allotted for the dorsal fin:

Length in relation to size	10 points
Form	10 points
Color	10 points

Forty points allotted for the caudal fin:

Length	15 points
Form	15 points
Color	10 points

The behavior and fin carriage of the fish could be awarded another 10 points, with a possible total of 100 points. Judges were admonished to evaluate in terms of specific percentages of the points available for any particular characteristic. For excellent, all points should be given; for very good, 8/10ths of the points; for good, 6/10ths of the points; for fair, 4/10ths of the points; for deficient, 2/10ths of the points, and for poor, no points at all. Body length was to be given a point score on its actual size:

2.8 cm and over	5 points
2.4 cm and over	3 points
1.8 cm and over	1 point.

As for form, the greatest depths should be at most a quarter of the body length, and the caudal base should be slender. Examples of deductible points:

	Deduct at least :
For plump caudal base	1 point
For a rounded back	2 points
Any sign of spinal curvature, hump back, alterations in shape as the result of disease or injury	No evaluation

The caudal fin length was rated by its proportion to the body length, measuring to the end of the caudal base, which lies up to within 3 mm of the forward edge of the caudal fin. The beginning of the dorsal fin base, situated close behind the middle of the body, was to be taken as a basic place for measuring the above figures. Only with single and double swords were the swords themselves to be taken into consideration. The length of the dorsal fin was to be rated by how far the end extended into the caudal fin region. The edges of the fins should be smooth, and the judges were warned not to let form and color interfere with each other when evaluating. Faulty form for instance, could be overlooked with the sword types if the transparent parts of the fins were not considered. Fantails may seem to have jagged fin edges merely because the color does not reach to the extremities. In the first case, there are faults in form, and in the second, the fault lies in the color.

The evaluation of color and markings was dependent particularly on the personal feelings of the judge, and it was felt that there could be no hard and fast rules. By the evaluations of several judges, each of whom gave his own opinion, it was expected to approach by the rules of probability an acceptable average taste on which the existence of judging rules usually rests. As a basis, the following formulations were given.

The color of a fish is judged by the area covered, and by the intensity of the colors; body and fins should be evenly covered in their full area with the same color pattern and intensity of colors. Breaks in a color surface in which the basic color shines through such as with a changed or striped pattern were not to be deterimental as long as they did not dominate and form an additional color pattern. Intensity of colors did not necessarily mean bright and sparkling colors; faint and subdued color tones such as greyish-blue or light lilac could be judged as intense if they were not dirty or washed-out. An unusual color and pattern could lead to the conclusion that it was the personal accomplishment of the breeder; this would be rated as excellent, and a full count of points would be given. A really good coloration without exceptional characteristics could get 6/10ths of the points, and colored pectoral fins could be given 2 extra points.

Behavior and fin carriage and the individual rating of swimming ability was intended to discourage over-breeding for exceptionally large finnage. The fish must be able to swim gracefully and swiftly with the fins functional; thus at least 2 points would be deducted for constantly hanging dorsal fins. For vigorous but snaky body motions, judges were to deduct at least 3 points; for constantly hanging caudal fins, at least 4 points, and for labored sluggish swimming, no evaluation was to be made.

If several entries were to be rated together, they should be similar in form and color. Small aberrations were to be permitted as long as the other properties of the fish gave them the generally similar appearance of being of one breed. An average was to be taken for fish exhibited together, not a scoring of the best fish as in the American system. With three fish of equally colored dorsal fins, if one had a different number of colored spots, a point would be deducted.

Thus the German standards were considerably more meticulous in detail than the American ones, and a good deal of figuring and calculating would have to be done by the judges in order to discover what conclusions to reach. Also a greater weight was given to the finnage, particularly to the caudal fin in overall judging, and a total of 35 points could be awarded for color as against 20 in the American scoring. Interestingly, we get the impression that the American breeders of later years have really been judging more to the German type than their own, with massive caudal fin development and high coloration as high scoring points. Also body size scores more heavily in the American field. Despite all this however it is apparent that both continental and American breeders have gone ahead and bred what seemed to them to be an attractive fish, whether or not it conformed particularly well to either set of standards, or to the earlier British standards, which do not seem to have been subject to any recent revision. This is considered to be a very sensible way of going about breeding, to take advantage of the genetic material which nature offers, to develop it by proved techniques to the fullest reasonable extent rather than to try forcing it into some preconceived notion of how a fish should appear. This is a sensible procedure and also likely to be much more successful. It is wise to keep in mind the unity of form and function that should lead to the graceful appearance of any living creature. Thus we would certainly agree that gross over-development of any particular feature should not be encouraged, and we do not wish to see in the guppy the type of development which has been established in the gold fish with telescopic eyes, curious appendages, and finnage which is clearly far too over-developed for functional purposes. At the same time it has to be admitted that even reasonably looking functional appearing guppies would have little chance of survival in nature, and thus all of our fancy fishbreeding is at least to some extent an artificiality.

12. STRAINS OF GUPPIES

Strains of colorful, long-finned guppies with large body size have been developed all over the world; centers of this development have however been primarily the United States and Britain. On the continent of Europe, developments came somewhat later but some of the most beautiful guppies in the world are now of Contintal origin; Often very similar guppy strains have been developed independently in different countries or by different breeders of a country and the exact relationship between these would be interesting in many cases to work out, but it has rarely been done.

Outstanding among guppy breeders is the name of Paul Hahnel; his guppies were large and beautifully colored and he worked for many years (until his death in 1969) in developing them. Myron Gordon gives an account of an interrogation of Paul Hahnel regarding the methods he used in producing his outstanding stocks. How much did he rely on a knowledge of genetics, and what importance did he attribute to feeding and rearing as against genetic constitution? Following this discussion, Gordon stated that Hahnel perhaps unconsciously did use the Mendelian principles of inheritance as a basis for his procedure, but he put great emphasis on the environmental conditions and provided his guppies with large tanks, clean tanks, clear water, good light, and plants. He felt strongly that the water sprite, a rapid-growing plant of the genus *Ceratopteris*, was one of the important factors in his success.

Another outstanding guppy breeder was William Sternke and following these stalwarts of the hobby have been many others who produced outstanding specimens. In general the producers of the first and still the most successful colorful, large finned, and large tailed breeds were the Americans; this is almost certainly because they departed from attempts to maintain rigid hypothetical standards and allowed nature to take a slightly-guided course, selecting the best from what was offered. The stocks in which these outstanding guppies have been produced have essentially been veiltail, delta-tail, or similar stocks, but within these a great variety of color variation and color pattern has been developed.

The British International Federation of Aquarium Societies was first to establish rules for the classification of guppies for exhibition, and these standards were used in early shows. They have been modified as we have noted by both German and American tables of standards, but the essence of the classification remains the same. The English breeders however stuck rather rigidly to some of the earlier types of guppy that were developed, as the swordtail, top or bottom sword, or double sword, the cofertail, or pintail, and produced beautifully shaped fishes which were not however very colorful. Even now the swordtail guppies bred from English stock tend to be rather colorless though very attractive in form.

Swordtail Guppies

The bottom-sword guppy with a straight sword-like extension of its tail fin and a somewhat elongated dorsal fin is a fairly frequent mutant in guppy stocks. It has not so far been produced in particularly attractive color varieties.

The top-sword guppy is similar to the bottom-sword except for the position of the sword, which is an extension of the upper section of the caudal fin. The same remarks apply to it as to the bottom-sword except that it is rather a rare fish.

The double-sword is difficult to achieve and the development of the two swords is in most cases unequal. A really evenly developed double-sword guppy is an outstanding prize winner. This guppy also has a somewhat elongated dorsal fin and may occur in a variety of colors but has not been produced in the brilliance of colors available in some of the later types.

Lyretails

The Lyretail guppy is a development of the swordtail type in which the tail fin is curved and lyre-shaped, with a long, upward curving dorsal fin. It seems to have been produced first in England and seldom occurs in outstanding color varieties.

Roundtails, Speartails, and Cofertails

These are all guppies with minor, if any, modifications of the normal round tail. Not much more need be said about them except that they are essentially long established British types without any great color variety usually to be found associated with them. They represent relatively early mutant forms which were fixed by the British aquarists and were so fixed at a time when other desirable characteristics of the guppy such as color and size were not particularly developed. Possibly nobody has thought it worthwhile to try to introduce large body size and intense coloration to these guppy types since they are not nearly as attractive as the large-tailed varieties upon which breeders have concentrated more recently.

Scarftails, Delta-tails, Fantails, Veiltails, and Others

These are the long tailed guppies, (usually with long dorsal fins of different shapes) upon which modern guppy breeding has focused. The scarftails or flagtails are

$3.95

guppy handbook

M. F. Roberts photo

by **DR. CLIFF W. EMMENS**
University of Sydney
Sydney, Australia

Published by T.F.H. Publications, P.O. Box 33, Jersey City, N.J. 07303. Distributed in England by T.F.H. (Gt. Britain) Ltd., 13 Nutley Lane, Reigate, Surrey, England. In Canada by Clarke, Irwin & Company Ltd., Clarwin House, 791 St. Clair Avenue West, Toronto 10, Ontario, Canada. To the book trade in the USA by Crown Publishers, Inc., 419 Park Avenue South, New York, N.Y. 10016.

Cover photo by Hilmar Hansen, Aquarium Berlin.

essentially fish possessing long ribbon-like tails bearing horizontal markings running more or less parallel with the dorsal fin and extending beyond the caudal base. Interestingly, the cross between the German emerald guppy and the fantail guppy results in a flagtail. The veiltail has a broader tail than the flagtail or scarftail, and broader still is the triangle or delta-tail. Triangles bred in America tend to have been called delta-tails rather than triangles. Various colors and color patterns, sometimes extremely attractive, have been developed in all of these types. It is difficult to produce uniformily colored guppies, in fact so difficult that no one has yet produced them, thus the tail and the fins will usually be of different color than the body. Reds have been produced with fairly reddish bodies as well, but uniform all-over coloration has yet to be produced in any color and breeders are still working on this problem.

Reclassification placing *Lebistes* and *Mollienisia* in the genus *Poecilia* makes the above guppy-molly cross a less rare hybrid that it was once considered. Dr. Eduard E. Schmidt photo.

13. PRIZE-WINNING GUPPIES

It is interesting to compare the show prize winners during an approximately ten year interval (1958–59 to 1968). From the illustrations in the *Tropical Fish Hobbyist* magazine for June 1960 in which an article by Dr. Eduard Schmidt described some of the first place winners in the international exhibitions held in Berlin and London in 1958 and in Bremen and London in 1959 comparisons may be made with the various first, second, and third prize winners in the Seventh International Guppy Show in Vienna in July 1968 and pictured in *TFH* magazine for November, 1968. Most of these were Viennese-bred fishes but some were sent from behind the Iron Curtain and a single batch of American fishes came from Mr. Joseph Bertagni of New York. The organizers of the show stated that Mr. Bertagni's guppies were the finest they had ever seen in respect to the intensive blue coloration and finnage, and his guppies gained more points than any others in the history of the Viennese shows, winning among many other prizes, the Best in Show award.

Swordtail and lyretail guppies of the earlier shows (1958 and 1959) were elegant, smallish, and pastel rather than brilliantly colored fish. The fish of the 1968 show were not very different; they were still pastel colored though they had in some cases rather more brilliant hues and markings in yellow and black that had not been seen previously. It is clear that the degree of development seen in some of the flowing-tailed fishes has not been realized even today in the simpler types.

The flagtails and fantails of earlier days were brilliant fish; they usually had variegated tails and even, when designated as red or some other color, they were certainly not uniformly colored. The body would characteristically be of a different color from the tail fin although the dorsal fin and tail fin might be similar. The outstanding contributors of these fish to the international shows of 1958 and 1959 were Rohrmoser of Germany (green flagtails and green fantails), Hahnel of the United States (prize winning red fantails), and Schutz and De Monte of Germany (varicolored fantails and veiltails, and blue triangles).

In the 1968 show, there were fish with considerably greater encroachment of the tail coloration onto the body, although there are still no doubt purposely-bred varieties in which the tail color is in sharp contrast to that of the body. The names of the breeders of these fishes are unfortunately not given, but in *TFH* magazine of November 1968 some beautiful golden fantails, bronze-green fantails, blue fantails, red fantails, and varicolored fantails are pictured. These prizewinning, very colorful guppies are more attractive than the earlier ones. Fish we have actually seen cannot be compared of course except in memory with those we saw a decade earlier, but the same impression (as from photographs) is conveyed—that great improvement has been made. Noticeable however is that there is no greater degree of caudal or dorsal fin development in these guppies than was seen earlier. However, we have seen considerably attractive non-prize winning guppy stocks with very much greater development of flowing tail than those that are the show winners. This is undoubtedly because of the rules which govern these shows and prevent a fish with excessive tail development from being awarded a prize. It seems doubtful whether quite such a rigid set of rules is desirable. Much the same prevails among the delta-tails or triangles. These fish have wider tails than the ones just discussed but the same inhibition has clearly been placed upon tail development. Body coloration in some of these fish is however very beautiful and undoubtedly shows advances on developments of the previous decade. Unfortunately, photographs of females of these strains are not available as it would be interesting to know to what extent these stocks carry color development in the females. We know this to have been achieved in a number of American stocks, but it is not clear whether the predominantly Viennese guppies which were award winners have also the same degree of development.

It might be illuminating to have a free-for-all guppy show in which there were no restrictions on the type entered and exhibitors would bc encouraged to submit whatever they considered to be beautiful guppies. Probably if freed of restrictions and not having to meet particular show standards, breeders might show some rather surprising fish. No doubt some of them would not be considered worth a second look by many a judge, but it is likely that some of the others would open the eyes of the public to what can be produced in the way of exotic finnage and exotic coloring in the once humble guppy. It should be realized, for instance, that the length of the tail in the guppy can reach about twice the body length, instead of being restricted as in the show standards to not exceeding the body length. Although the possessors of such enormous finnage are certainly slowed in their body movements, their progress through the water can only be described as graceful if the fish is in good condition and its finnage is of a balanced conformation.